New and Collected Poems
for Children

Poet Laureate

CAROL ANN DUFFY

New and Collected Poems for Children

Illustrated by Alice Stevenson

faber and faber

First published in 2009
by Faber and Faber Limited
Bloomsbury House, 74–77 Great Russell Street, London WC1B 3DA

Design by Mandy Norman
Printed in England by TJ International Ltd, Padstow, Cornwall

Poems © Carol Ann Duffy, 1999, 2000, 2003, 2007, 2009
Illustrations © Alice Stevenson, 2009

The right of Carol Ann Duffy to be identified as author of this work, and Alice
Stevenson as illustrator of this work, has been asserted in accordance with Section 77
of the Copyright, Designs and Patents Act 1988

A CIP record for this book
is available from the British Library

ISBN 978–0–571–21968–1

2 4 6 8 10 9 7 5 3 1

for Ella with love from Mummy

Contents

The Words of Poems	1
Meeting Midnight	3
Late	4
Lies	5
Prior Knowledge	7
Know All	8
The Oldest Girl in the World	9
Rooty Tooty	12
Your Grandmother	13
The Good Child's Guide to Rock'n'Roll	14
The Who?	23
Elvis Lives	24
Boys	25
Five Girls	27
Brave Dave	29
Jemima Riddle	30
Questions, Questions	31
How Many Sailors to Sail a Ship?	32
The Ocean's Blanket	35
Sand	36
Poker	37
Queens	38
The Duke of Fire and the Duchess of Ice	41
Three	42
The Giantess	43
Sharp Freckles	44
A Bad Princess	45
The Scottish Prince	46
Vows	47
The Loch Ness Monster's Husband	49
Henrietta, The Eighth	50
Queen's Bees	51

The Wasp 52

Moth 53

A Stick Insect's Funeral Poem 54

The Birds, the Fish and the Insects 55

Tight 65

Snide 66

Seven Deadly Adjectives 68

Fine Weather 75

Little Ghost 76

Touched 78

Don't Be Scared 79

Boo! to a Goose 80

Be Very Afraid 81

Quicksand 83

A Worry 84

Whirlpool 86

Tales of the Expected 87

The Childminders 89

The Babysitter 90

Beebop Da Beebop 93

The Manchester Cows 95

The Great Bed of Ware 100

Song 102

The Song Collector 103

Johann Sebastian Baa 104

His Nine Sympathies 105

A Child's Song 106

Spell 107

Teacher 108

Mrs Hamilton's Register 109

The Laugh of Your Class 110

I Adore Year 3 112

The Alphabest 113

Your School 115

The Fruits, the Vegetables, the Flowers and the Trees 117

Cucumbers 131

Halo 132

Numbers 134

_/_/99 139

In Nineteen Ninety-nine 140

Counting to a Billion 141

Zero 146

The Moon 149

The Good Friend of Melanie Moon 151

Friends 153

Brave Enough 155

Girl and Tree 156

A Crow and a Scarecrow 157

The Glove 159

Gifts 161

Ask Oscar 164

A Rhyme 166

Translation 168

Dimples 169

Irish Rats Rhymed to Death 170

Opposites 172

The Sock 173

Crikey Dick 174

Not Not Nursery Rhymes 175

Inside the Egg 177

F for Fox 182

Nippy Maclachlan 183

Ran Out of Sugar 184

Toy Dog 186

Begged 187

There's a Dog 189

Glad 191

So Shy 192

♫ ♫   193
Chocs   194
Fishcakes   195
Grandma Barr's Cherry Tomatoes   197
Was a Lad   199
The Red Skeleton   201
Cuddling Skeletons   202
Skeleton, Moon, Poet   203
Going On the Web   205
Safe Sounds   208
Sweet Homes   209
Secrets   211
Star and Moon   212
First Summer   213
Time Transfixed *by René Magritte*   214
Pestle and Mortar   215
Al Ponte dei Giocattoli / The Bridge of Toys   216
Please   217
Your Dresses   219
Perhaps   220
The Look   221
Pay Me in Light   222
Loving   223
Whee!   224
Lost   225
Jamjar   226
The Thief, the Priest and the Golden Coin   227
The Theft   228
Snowball   229
Walk   231
Don't Go to China   232
The Invention of Rain   233
How Emily Mercer (96) Grew Young   234
Lightning Star   235

The Maiden Names   236
Peggy Guggenheim   237
Venezia   238
The Famous   239
Deal with It   240
Moon   241
Elvis! Shakespeare! Picasso! Virginia Woolf!   242
The Hat   243
Picasso's Blue Paintings   248
The Architect of Cheese   253
A Week as My Home Town   255
The Rings   258
The Written Queen   259
Haikus from Basho   260
No Stone Unturned   262
A Child's Sleep   269
Night Writing   270

The Words of Poems

The words of poems are nails
which tack the wind to a page,
so that the gone hour
when your kite pulled you over the field
blows in your hair.

They're hand-mirrors, a poem's words,
holding the wept tears on your face,
like a purse holds small change, or the breath
that said things.

They're fishing-nets,
scooping sprats and tiddlers out of a stream
or the gleaming trout that startled the air
when you threw it back. The words of poems

are stars, dot-to-dots of the Great Bear,
the Milky Way your telescope caught; or breves
filled with the light of the full moon you saw
from your bedroom window; or little flames
like the tongues of Hallowe'en candles.

The words of poems are spells, dropping
like pennies into a wishing-well, remember
the far splash? They're sparklers,
scrawling their silver loops and hoops
on the night, again in your gloved fist
on November the Fifth.

They're goldfish
in their sad plastic bags at the fair,
you stood there. The words of poems
are coins in a poor man's hat; the claws of a lost cat.
The words of poems are who you were.

Meeting Midnight

I met Midnight.
Her eyes were sparkling pavements after frost.
She wore a full-length, dark-blue raincoat with a hood.
She winked. She smoked a small cheroot.

I followed her.
Her walk was more a shuffle, more a dance.
She took the path to the river, down she went.
On Midnight's scent,
I heard the twelve cool syllables, her name,
chime from the town.
When those bells stopped,

Midnight paused by the water's edge.
She waited there.
I saw a girl in purple on the bridge.
It was One o'Clock.
Hurry, Midnight said. *It's late, it's late.*
I saw them run together.
Midnight wept.
They kissed full on the lips
and then I slept.

The next day I bumped into Half-Past Four.
He was a bore.

Late

She was eight. She was out late.
She bounced a tennis ball homewards before her
                    in the last of the light.
She'd been warned. She'd been told. It grew cold.
She took a shortcut through the churchyard.
She was a small child
making her way home. She was quite brave.
She fell into an open grave.

It was deep. It was damp. It smelled strange.
Help, she cried, *Help, it's Me!* She shouted
                    her own name.
Nobody came.
The churchbells tolled sadly. Shame. Shame.

She froze. She had a blue nose.
She clapped her hands.
She stamped her feet in soft, slip-away soil.
She hugged herself. Her breath was a ghost
                    floating up from a grave.
Then she prayed.

But only the moon stared down
                    with its callous face.
Only the spiteful stars sniggered, far out in space.
Only the gathering clouds
threw down a clap of thunder
like an ace.
And her, she was eight, going on nine.
She was late.

Lies

I like to go out for the day and tell lies.
The day should be overcast
with a kind of purple, electric edge to the clouds;
and not too hot or cold,
but cool.
I turn up the collar of my coat
and narrow my eyes.

I meet someone –
a girl from school perhaps –
I like them shy.
Then I start to lie
as we walk along Tennyson Drive kicking a can.
She listens hard,
her split strawberry mouth moist and mute;
my weasel words
sparking the little lights in her spectacles.
At the corner of Coleridge Place
I watch her run,
thrilled, fast, chasing her breath,
home to her mum.

Bus-stops I like,
with long, bored, footsore, moaning queues.
I lie to them
in my shrill, confident voice,
till the number 8 or 11 takes them away
and I stand and stare at the bend in Longfellow Road,
alone in the day.

At the end of the darkening afternoon
I head for home,
watching the lights turn on in truthful rooms
where mothers come and go
with plates of cakes,
and TV sets shuffle their bright cartoons.
Then I knock on the door of 21 Wordsworth Way,
and while I wait
I watch a spaceship zoom away overhead
and see the faint half-smile of the distant moon.
They let me in.
And who, they want to know, do I think I am?
Exactly where have I been? With whom? And why?
The thing with me –
I like to come home after a long day out
and lie.

Prior Knowledge

Prior Knowledge was a strange boy.
He had sad green eyes.
He always seemed to know when I was telling lies.

We were friends for a summer.
Prior got out his knife
and mixed our bloods so we'd be brothers for life.

You'll be rich, he said, and famous;
but I must die.
Then brave, clever Prior began to cry.

He knew so much.
He knew the day before
I'd drop a jamjar full of frogspawn on the kitchen floor.

He knew there were wasps
in the gardening gloves.
He knew the name of the girl I'd grow up to love.

The day he died
he knew there would be
a wind shaking conkers from the horse-chestnut tree;

and an aimless child
singing down Prior's street,
with bright red sandals on her skipping feet.

Know All

I know something you don't know.
I know what you mean.
I know what's going on round here.
I know what I've seen.
I know the score.
I know a lot more
than folk give me credit for.
I know what's what.
I know a lot.
I know all that.

I know the lay of the land.
I know it like I know
the back of my own hand.
I know enough.
I know my stuff.
I know what you're saying.
I know which way the wind
is blowing.
I know what to do.
I know who's who.

I know the ropes.
I know the ins and outs.
I know my onions.
I know what folk are on about.
I know beyond a shadow of a doubt –

I DON'T KNOW NOWT.

The Oldest Girl in the World

Children, I remember how I could hear
with my soft young ears
the tiny sounds of the air –
tinkles and chimes
like minuscule bells
ringing continually there;
clinks and chinks
like glasses of sparky gooseberry wine,
jolly and glinting and raised in the air.
Yes, I could hear like a bat. And how!
Can't hear a sniff of it now.

Truly, believe me, I could all the time see
every insect that crawled in a bush,
every bird that hid in a tree,
individually.
If I wanted to catch a caterpillar
to keep as a pet in a box
I had only to watch a cabbage
and there it would be,
crawling bendy and green towards me.
Yes, I could see with the eyes of a cat. Miaow!
Can't see a sniff of it now.

And my sense of taste was second to none.
By God, the amount I knew with my tongue!
The shrewd taste of a walnut's brain.
The taste of a train from a bridge.
Of a kiss. Of air chewy with midge.
Of fudge from a factory two miles away
from the house where I lived.
I'd stick out my tongue
to savour the sky in a droplet of rain.
Yes, I could taste like the fang of a snake. Wow!
Can't taste a sniff of it now.

On the scent, what couldn't I smell
with my delicate nose, my nostrils of pearl?
I could smell the world!
Snow. Soot. Soil.
Satsumas snug in their Christmas sock.
The ink of a pen.
The stink of an elephant's skin.
The blue broth of a swimming-pool. Dive in!
The showbizzy gasp of the wind.
Yes, I could smell like a copper's dog. Bow-wow!
Can't smell a sniff of it now.

As for my sense of touch
it was too much!
The cold of a snowball
felt through the vanishing heat of a mitt.
A peach like an apple wearing a vest.
The raffia dish of a bird's nest.
A hot chestnut
branding the palm at the heart of the fist.
The stab of the thorn on the rose. Long grass, its itch.
Yes, I could feel with the sensitive hand of a ghost. Whooo!
Can't feel a sniff of it now.

Can't see a
Can't hear a
Can't taste a
Can't smell a
Can't feel a bit of it whiff of it niff of it.
Can't get a sniff of it now.

Rooty Tooty

Grandad used to be a pop star,
with a red-and-silver guitar.
He wore leather jackets and drainpipe jeans.
He drove around in limousines,
waving to screaming fans.
Fab! said Grandad. *Groovy!*
I really dig it, man!

Grandad used to have real hips,
he swivelled and did The Twist.
His record went to Number One.
Grandad went like this:
Rooty tooty, yeah yeah.
Rooty tooty, yeah yeah.
Rooty tooty, yeah yeah.
Then Grandad met Gran.

Gran was dancing under a glitterball.
Grandad was on bass.
He noticed how a thousand stars
sparkled and shone in her face.
And although Gran fancied the drummer,
Grandad persevered. He wrote Gran
a hundred love songs
down through their happy years.

Grandad used to be a pop star,
a rock'n'roll man –
Rooty tooty, yeah yeah yeah –
and Grandad loved groovy Gran.

Your Grandmother

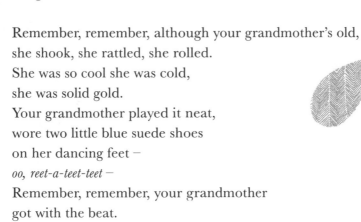

Remember, remember, there's many a thing
your grandmother doesn't dig
if it ain't got that swing;
many a piece of swag
she won't pick up and put in her bag
if it seems like a drag.
She painted it red – the town –
she lassooed the moon.
Remember, remember, your grandmother
boogied on down.

Remember, remember, although your grandmother's old,
she shook, she rattled, she rolled.
She was so cool she was cold,
she was solid gold.
Your grandmother played it neat,
wore two little blue suede shoes
on her dancing feet –
oo, reet-a-teet-teet –
Remember, remember, your grandmother
got with the beat.

Remember, remember, it ain't what you do
it's the way that you do it.
Your grandmother knew it –
she had a balloon and she blew it,
she had a ball
and was belle of it
just for the hell of it.
She was Queen of the night.
Remember, remember, your grandmother's
aaaaaaaaaaaaallllllll riiiiiiiiiiiiiiight.

The Good Child's Guide to Rock'n'Roll

1 BILL HALEY (1925–81)

In a bright check jacket
and kiss-curl hair,
plump Bill Haley
was debonair.

One, two, three o'clock,
four o'clock, ROCK . . .
Bill boogied in his creepers
and his spangly socks,

A friendly gnome
with a fat guitar,
Bill Haley was a jolly old
rock'n'roll star.

2 FATS DOMINO (b.1928)

Fats tickled the ivories
in New Orleans,
he was full of boogie-woogie,
he was full of beans.

Dominus, dominum, domine,
DOMINO!
Ten fast fingers,
look at them go.

Fats was a piano man
who found his thrill
in a faraway place
called Blueberry Hill.

Dominus, dominum, domine,
DOMINO!
Ten smart fingers
on the pi-an-oh.

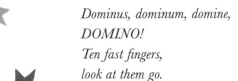

3 LITTLE RICHARD (*b.*1932)

Little Richard
was a twitcher,
a squealer,
an *Oo Luciller*,
a whooper
and a hollerer,
a bet your bottom dollarer,
banging
the joanna
with the heels of his shoes –
a wop bop a loo bop
a wop bam boom!

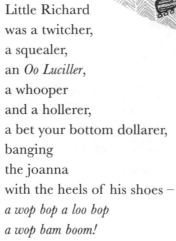

4 CHUCK BERRY (*b.*1926)

Chuck walked like a duck
as he strummed his axe,
scooting round the stage
going *quacketty quack*,
singing *Johnny B. Goode*
and *Maybellene*,
singing like a bird,
playing like a dream –
Rock'n'Roll Music,
Sweet Little Sixteen –
Chuck Berry was a jumping
human bean.

5 ELVIS PRESLEY (1935–77)

Elvis was King,
he swivelled
his hips, wore
drainpipe jeans
with gold zips,
sang, danced,
pouted, sneered –
You ain't nothin'
but a hound dog –
bowed, dis-
appeared. Elvis
was King, drove
a pink Cadillac,
drank ice-cream soda
in the back.
His Mama said
her boy done well,
Elvis sang
Heartbreak Hotel,
died too young
still the King,
now the angels
hear him sing –
Love me tender,
love me true,
tapping on his cloud
with a blue
suede shoe.

6 BO DIDDLEY (1928–2008)

Bo Diddley
got fiddly
on a diddley bow.

Rhythm & blues
in his fingers
and toes.

*I shall
have music
wherever I go.*

Bo Diddley
got fiddly
on a diddley bow.

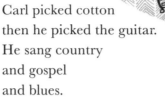

7 CARL PERKINS (1932–98)

Carl picked cotton
then he picked the guitar.
He sang country
and gospel
and blues.

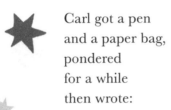

He played at a dance,
heard a dude
tell a doll
not to step
on his blue suede shoes.

Carl got a pen
and a paper bag,
pondered
for a while
then wrote:

*Well, it's one
    for the money.
        Two for the show.
            Three to get ready.
                Now go . . .*

19

8 THE EVERLY BROTHERS
(Don, *b.*1937; Phil, *b.*1939)

The Everly boys,
Phil and Don,
in their cradle
sang a song.

Record labels
came along,
made showbiz stars
of Phil and Don.

Little Susie,
Cathy's Clown,
Phil and Don
got on down –

sweetly chiming
in their song,
neatly rhyming,
Phil and Don.

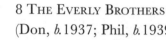
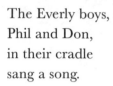
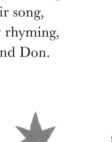
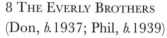

9 JERRY LEE LEWIS (*b.*1935)

Verily,
Jerry Lee
merrily
boogied,
his voice
screaming
higher
and higher.
Cheerily
Jerry Lee
leerily
woogied,
goodness
gracious
great balls
of fire!

10 BUDDY HOLLY (1936–59)

Buddy and his Crickets
could hiccup and chirp,
play for Peggy Sue
in her dancing skirt.

Buddy and his Crickets –
That'll Be The Day.
Peggy Sue, Peggy Sue –
Not Fade Away.

Buddy and his Crickets
caught an aeroplane,
now poor Peggy Sue
won't dance again.

Buddy and his Crickets –
That'll Be The Day.
Peggy Sue, Peggy Sue –
Not Fade Away.

Buddy and his Crickets –
guitar, drums, bass –
sing to Peggy Sue
from a star in space.

Buddy and his Crickets –
That'll Be The Day.
Peggy Sue, Peggy Sue,
Not Fade Away.

The Who?

It came as a big surprise to me to find
that someone as ancient as you
has a favourite band
or *group* as you tell me now
they were called back then.
What? Where? Which? Why? When?
The Who?

You slide in a video
and sit with a silly smile on your face
at the flickering black-and-white
of your ghostly and ghastly past.
What do you mean
What a blast!
Why do you shout
Far out!
and gaze at the man with the blue guitar
as though he were God?
Read my lips –
he's odd.
His arm's like a broken windmill
blown away by a hurricane.
Look at his pompous big-nosed face.
Look at his awful clothes.
You sad case.

The what? The *Who*?
Who cares how many records
went to gold.
I hope they die before they get old.

Elvis Lives

Elvis lives.
He's in my class at school.
He's cool.
He walks across the playground,
swirls his hips.
He sings hymns in assembly,
curls his lip.

Elvis is alive
and well.
He took a piece of chalk
and on the blackboard
while the teacher took a walk
wrote out the lyrics of
Heartbreak Hotel.

Elvis talks.
He did not die.
He's top in Maths.
He's good at swimming, French and cookery,
good for a laugh.
He wears school uniform, school tie,
school blue suede shoes.
He keeps his head down when he's got the blues

or, by the bike shed,
plays an air guitar.
Love Me Tender
on the playground air.
My best friend, Elvis Presley, with his slicked-back hair.

Boys

1 PAUL

I wake early, gargle with my bells
to shake out birds from my stone curls.
My thoughts are gargoyles.

I can see the river with my stained-glass eyes,
the boats and barges floating like ideas.
My huge forehead frowns in London skies.

I'm cold, but I do not mind the cold.
Far away, I hear the stammered prayers of the healed.
Far away, I hear the baptised crying of a child.

2 OSCAR

Give me the hands of Marlon Brando.
Give me the neck of Gregory Peck.
Give me the smile of Robert de Niro.
Give me the brain of John Wayne.

Give me the eyes of Bette Davis.
Give me the hair of Cher.
Give me the legs of Betty Grable.
Give me it all one more time. I was there.

3 STANLEY

I'm a flashing blade, I'm a knave.
A fork's my wife.
I'll make my point – enough's enough.
I'll cut up rough.
I'll cut your coat according to your cloth.
I'll cut no ice.
Cross me, you're blind, dumb, deaf,
a stiff.
I'll have your life,
like this, quick – *Knife* . . .

4 GORDON BENNETT

Is it uncouth?
Is it a fate worse than death?
Is it like coal in the bath?

Is it a kick in the teeth?
Is it a just cause for wrath?
Is it like having bad breath?

When your ****** *** name is a ****** **** oath.

5 BEN

I'm big,
bigger than fifty men.
I go Dong! Dong! Dong! Dong! Dong!
Dong! Dong! Dong! Dong! Dong!
on *News at Ten*.

Five Girls

Philomena Cooney
wears green sandals,
yellow ribbons,
silver bangles;
knows three secrets,
lives in a tent
in the middle of a field
near the River Trent.

Arabella Murkhi
speaks in Latin,
keeps her cat in,
sleeps in satin.
Went to Turkey
just like that.
Absolutely *loved* it.
Amo amas amat.

Isadora Dooley
loves her jewellery.
Pearls on Sundays,
diamonds Mondays,
rubies Tuesdays,
Wednesdays blue days,
Thursday Friday Saturdays
it-doesn't-really-matter days.

Esther Feaver,
opera diva
dressed in beaver,
loved a weaver;
took a breather,
grabbed a cleaver,
now the weaver
will not leave her.

Joan Stone
liked a good moan,
lived on her own
in a mobile home.
The doorbell never rang,
neither did the phone;
so she pressed her ear
to the dialling tone.

Brave Dave

Brave Dave lived on his own in a cave. He liked a good rave; he raved till the wee small hours, waving and dancing, but he craved company. One day, there was a knock on the door of Thin Lyn's tin. Thin Lyn was slim as a pin and lived alone in said tin, swigging pink gin from a thimble. She liked to play cards and win. Snap! 'Do me a favour,' said Brave Dave to Thin Lyn, 'And come to the cave for a rave.' She gave him a trim grin. 'Before we begin the thing, we must ask Vain Jane.' Vain Jane was a pain. She lived up a lane in A Room Of One's Ain and spoke posh. Nevertheless, Brave Dave and Thin Lyn walked up the lane to invite Vain Jane to the rave in the cave. Having checked for rain, Vain Jane deigned to accept – nothing venture, nothing gain – but insisted they call on Well-Bred Fred at his shed on the way. Alas! Well-Bred Fred was dead, having choked on a crust of bread, fallen and bumped his head, which had bled, all red. Vain Jane went insane. Brave Dave dug a grave, and Thin Lyn drank pink gin. Tears dripped from the end of her chin.

Jemima Riddle

A:
Jemima Riddle
plays the fiddle,
hey-diddle-diddle
d.

B:
D'you think the kid'll
play the middle
bit of it at
t?

A:
No. Jemima Riddle'
d rather piddle,
hey-diddle-diddle –
d.

B:
P?

A:
Oui. But a quid'll
stop the widdle,
then she'll fiddle –
C?

Questions, Questions

Why is my shadow copying me?
Because you are right.
Why do bananas smile in their bowl?
Because of your kind bite.

Why is the moon following me?
Because of your p-p-peep.
Why do the stars giggle at me?
Because of your h-h-hop.

Why do the trees gossip and nudge?
Because you are News.
How shall I find my way home in the dark?
By the light of your yellow shoes.

How Many Sailors
to Sail a Ship?

One with a broken heart
to weep sad buckets.

Two with four blue eyes
to mirror the sea.

One with a salty tongue
to swear at a pirate.

Two with four green eyes
to mirror the sea.

One with a wooden leg
to dance on a gang-plank.

Two with four grey eyes
to mirror the sea.

Luff! Leech! Clew! Tack!
Off to sea! Won't be back!

One with an arrowed heart
tattooed on a bicep.

Two with four blue eyes
to mirror the sky.

One with a baby's caul
to keep from a-drowning.

Two with four grey eyes
to mirror the sky.

One with a flask of rum
to gargle at midnight.

Two with four black eyes
to mirror the sky.

Luff! Clew! Tack! Leech!
Off to sea! No more beach!

One with an albatross
to put in a poem.

Two with four blue eyes
to mirror the sea.

One with a secret map
to stitch in a lining.

Two with four grey eyes
to mirror the sea.

One with a violin
to scrape at a dolphin.

Two with four green eyes
to mirror the sea.

Luff! Leech! Tack! Clew!
Off to sea! Yo ho! Adieu!

One with a telescope
to clock the horizon.

Two with four blue eyes
to mirror the sky.

One with a yard of rope
to lasso a tempest.

Two with four grey eyes
to mirror the sky.

One with a heavy heart
to sink for an anchor.

Two with four black eyes
to mirror the sky.

Leech! Clew! Tack! Luff!
Off to sea! We've had enough!
Luff! Leech! Tack! Clew!
Off to sea! Yo ho! Adieu!

The Ocean's Blanket

The ocean's blanket is made of dark green seaweed
and golden mermaids' hair.
We see a thousand starfish there.

The ocean's blanket is made of crashing waves
and frothy, creamy foam.
It keeps us warm.

The ocean's blanket is made of smiling dolphins
and lonely, singing whales.
We see the silver of the fishes' scales.

The ocean's blanket is made of waltzing octopuses
and dancing, inky squid.
It keeps us hid.

The ocean's blanket is made of hidden pearls
and spicy, salty smells.
We see the jewels of a million shells.

The ocean's blanket is made of sunken ships
and we are drowned, are drowned.
Beneath the ocean's blanket we will not be found.

Sand

I believe in sand
because of its thousand whispers
held in my hands,

because of a starfish
worn like a brooch
and earring shells,

and the way it frowns
when the tide goes out,
and its seaweed smell.

I believe in sand
because of its magic castle
made by my hands,

because of a name
scored with a stick
at the edge of the tide,

and the salty lace
at the throat of a wave
where dolphins ride.

I believe in sand
because of the secret water
dug by my hands,

because of the footprints
leading away, leading away
to other lands,
I believe in sand.

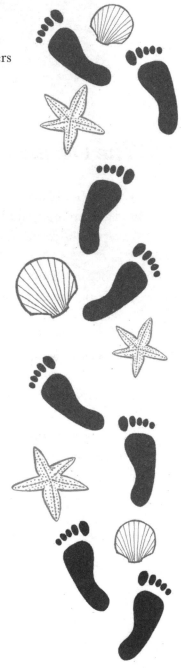

Poker

A skeleton
on the sea-bed,
a bullet-hole
in its bone head.

Three queens
in its claw hand,
a black ace
on the pale sand.

A fish swims
near a fourth queen
where a shirt sleeve
would once have been.

Queens

A cold, bored Queen lived in a castle.
She was Queen as far as the castle walls,
no farther.
Rooks flapped about. HM stared out from the East tower
in her blue robes, in the dull old gold of her crown;
a thin white Queen with grey-green eyes under a tight frown.

She wrote to a second Queen; she penned a formal letter
with a clammy candlewax seal. *I hope
you are feeling better. Please come.*
For three days, a man on a black horse
rode uphill with the letter.
For two days, he rode downhill with the answer.
Very well. Very well.
A trembling royal hand reached out, tugged
at the hanging rope of the servants' bell.

Queen Two was fat, with a loud voice
and a temper.
She dressed in a piccalilli yellow.
Queen One came down to greet her
in the Great Pink Hall for dinner.
Clear soup. Spinach. Fish.
What's this? the big Queen bellowed,
Rubbish to make me thinner?
Where is the curry, the pepper, the pickle,
the onion, the mustard and chilli?
Where is the garlic bread?
I'm off to bed.

At daybreak, a quiet Queen sat by her chessboard,
pale, apprehensive, fainter of heart.
A cross Queen thumped in, unthin.
What's going on? Where are the boxing-gloves,
the duelling swords, the snooker cues, where are the darts?
The rooks outside were alarmed, cawed back
at her deafening shout –
I'M GOING OUT!

That night, Queen One mooted a walk
in the castle grounds.
It was mild. There was a moon up above
and a moon in the moat.
They could stroll, calm, polite, Queen hand in Queen glove,
under the yews, the ancient oaks.
Is this a joke? Queen Two snapped.
Where are the bagpipes, the fiddlers three,
where is the karaoke? Answer me that!
TAXI!

So both Queens tried harder, harder.
Queen Thin let Queen Fat
raid the royal larder.
Fat held Thin's wool,
her big, plump, soft regal hands
frozen mid-clap.
Queen Thin knitted away, click, click-clack, click-clack.
Then both Queens sat in a marble bath –
Fat at the bottom, Thin by the taps –

We are clean Queens, they sang,
We are fragrant.
We are very very very clean Queens.

And when it was time,
Queen One managed a slight bow of the head,
Queen Two shuffled the start of a curtsy
under her dress.
Farewell, farewell,
a fat Queen called from a gold coach,
trotting away down the gravel drive, over the moat,
a big puce Queen
with a string of rubies at her throat.
Goodbye, goodbye.

Goodbye. A thin Queen waved from a window, shyly,
then fingered her new pearls.
One two three four five six seven.
Seven rooks round a castle started to cry.

The Duke of Fire
and the Duchess of Ice

Passionate love for the Duke of Fire
the Duchess of Ice felt.
One kiss was her heart's desire,
but with one kiss she would melt.

She dreamed of him in his red pantaloons,
in his orange satin blouse,
in his crimson cravat,
in his tangerine hat,
in his vermilion dancing shoes.

One kiss, one kiss,
lips of flame on frost,
one kiss, pure bliss,
and never count the cost.

She woke. She went to the bathroom.
She took a freezing shower –
her body as pale as a stalagmite,
winter's frailest flower.

Then the Duke of Fire stood there,
radiant, ablaze with love,
and the Duchess of Ice cared nothing
for anything in the world.

She spoke his name,
her voice was snow,
kissed him, kissed him again,
and in his warm, passionate arms
turned to water, tears, rain.

Three

I met a miniature King
by the side of the road,
wearing a crown
and an ermine suit –
important, small,
plump as a natterjack toad.
Kneel! he shrieked, *Kneel for the King!*
Certainly not, I said,
I'll do no such thing.

I saw a Giantess,
tall as a tree.
You'll do for a doll, she bellowed,
just the toy for me!
Into the box! Scream hard! Scream long!
I stared at her mad pond eyes
then skipped away.
Dream on . . .

I bumped into an Invisible Boy – *ouch!* –
at the edge of the field.
Give me a chocolate drop
said a voice.
What do you say? said I.
Please.
So I did
then stared as it floated mid-air
and melted away.

These are three of the people I met yesterday.

The Giantess

Where can I find seven small girls to be pets,
where can I find them?
One to comb the long grass of my hair
with this golden rake,
one to dig with this copper spade
the dirt from under my nails.
I will pay them in crab-apples.

Where can I find seven small girls to help me,
where can I find them?
A third to scrub at my tombstone teeth
with this mop in its bronze bucket,
a fourth to scoop out the wax from my ears
with this platinum trowel.
I will pay them in yellow pears.

Where can I find seven small girls to be good dears,
where can I find them?
A fifth one to clip the nails of my toes
with these sharp silver shears,
a sixth to blow my enormous nose
with this satin sheet.
I will pay them in plums.

But the seventh girl will stand on the palm of my hand,
singing and dancing,
and I will love the tiny music of her voice,
her sweet little jigs.
I will pay her in grapes and kumquats and figs.
Where can I find her?
Where can I find seven small girls to be pets?

Sharp Freckles

for Ben Simmons

He picks me up, his big thumbs under my armpits tickle,
then puts me down. On his belt there is a shining silver buckle.
I hold his hand and see, close up, the dark hairs on his knuckles.

He sings to me. His voice is loud and funny and I giggle.
Now we will eat. I listen to my breakfast as it crackles.
He nods and smiles. His eyes are birds in little nests of wrinkles.

We kick a ball, red and white, between us. When he tackles
I'm on the ground, breathing a world of grass. It prickles.
He bends. He lifts me high above his head. Frightened, I wriggle.

Face to his face, I watch the sweat above each caterpillar-eyebrow trickle.
He rubs his nose on mine, once, twice, three times, and we both chuckle.
He hasn't shaved today. He kisses me. He has sharp freckles.

A Bad Princess

A Bad Princess stomped through the woods
in a pair of boots
                    looking for trouble –
diamond tiara, satin dress, hair an absolute mess,
ready to bubble.

Imagine her shock and surprise
when she bumped straight into
                            her very own double:
a Tree Girl,
with shiny holly-green eyes
and a crown of autumn leaves on her wild head,
the colour of both of their hair.

Don't you dare, screamed Bad,
walk in these Royal woods looking like me!

I shall do as I please, you grumpy old thing,
said Tree.
Give me those emeralds that hang from your ears
or I'll kick you hard
and pinch you meanly.
Then we'll see which one of we two
is cut out
            to be Queenly!

Oh! The Bad Princess turned
                            and ran,
ran for her life
into the arms of the dull young Prince
and became his wife.

The Scottish Prince

Every summer, I visit the Scottish Prince
at his castle high on a hill outside Crieff.
We dine on haggis and tatties and neeps –
I drink water with mine and the Prince sips
at a peaty peppery dram. Then it's time for the dance.

O Scottish Prince, the heathery air sweetens the night.
Bats hang upside down in the pines like lamps waiting
for light. Ask me, ask me to dance to the skirl o' the pipes.

All the girls are in dresses. The boys are in kilts,
but no boy's so fine as the Prince in his tartan pleats.
I wait for a glance from the Prince, for the chance
to prance or flounce by his side, to bounce hand in hand
down the Gay Gordon line. *Och, the pleasure's a' mine!*

O Scottish Prince, the heathery air sweetens the night.
Bats hang upside down in the pines like lamps waiting
for light. Ask me, ask me to dance to the skirl o' the pipes.

At the end of summer, I say goodbye to the Scottish Prince
and catch a train to the South, over the border, the other side
of the purple hills, far from the blue and white flag, waving farewell
from the castle roof. The Prince will expect me back again
next year – here's a sprig of heather pressed in my hand as proof.

O Scottish Prince, the heathery air sweetens the night.
Bats hang upside down in the pines like lamps waiting
for light. Ask me, ask me to dance to the skirl o' the pipes.
Ask me, ask me, ask me to dance to the skirl o' the pipes.

Vows

1. BRIDE

I will not marry a Duke
who walks like a duck.
I will not marry an Earl
who feels like an eel.
I will not marry a Knight
who jumps like a gnat.

I will not marry a Chap
who looks like a chip.
I will not marry a Cove
who lives in a cave.
I will not marry a Bloke
with a brain like a brick.

I will not marry a Copper
who talks like a kipper.
I will not marry a Tenor
who sings like a tuna.
I will not marry a Poet
who squawks like a parrot.

2. GROOM

I will not marry a Dame
who dwells in a dome.
I will not marry a Hon
who broods like a hen.
I will not marry a Duchess
who paddles in ditches.

I will not marry a Maiden
who mings like a midden.
I will not marry a Lass
who bites like a louse.
I will not marry a Girl
who glares like a ghoul.

I will not marry a Lawyer
with the tongue of a liar.
I will not marry a Cook
who crows like a cock.
I will not marry a Painter
who snarls like a panther.

3. BOTH

So we will marry each other
and save all the bother.

The Loch Ness Monster's Husband

for Ella and her Dad

She's real. Ah married her and we bide
in the Loch. No weans. Ah'm a wee guy,
but she's big as a legend, all monster, the one
who swims the dark wet miles to the surface
and sticks her neck oot. Ah thought love
was only true in fairy tales, but Ah went
for a dip one day and saw her face. Now,
Ah'm a believer.

Henrietta, The Eighth

First one bored one,
off with his head.

Second one lazy,
better off dead.

Third one crazy,
rack for a bed.

Fourth one crossed one,
poisoned his drink.

Fifth one told lies,
stones made him sink.

Sixth one, old guy,
went in a blink.

Seventh one bugged one,
swung from a rope.

Eighth one right one,
one hope.

Queen's Bees

*In Elizabethan times, it was considered lucky to tell
bees gossip otherwise they would leave.*

The Queen told the bees
it was Henry VIII she mourned.
Grieving, they swarmed.

The Queen told the bees
of the axe at the throat of her mother.
They swooned in the clover.

The Queen told the bees
there was no man living she'd love.
Smitten, they buzzed.

The Queen told the bees
the names of those sent to the Tower.
They prayed at their flowers.

The Queen told the bees
of the rack, the thumbscrew, the whip.
Frenzied, they sipped.

The Queen told the bees
that the head of Queen Mary had fallen.
They cheered and huzzahed in the pollen.

The Wasp

Help me to love the wasp,
help me to do that thing –
to admire the raspy buzz
of its wings, to grow fond
of its droning whinge.

Help me to clasp the wasp
to my breast, or at least
to train it to jump from my finger
to thumb, a stripy pet,
to get it to fetch, to stand up

and beg, waving two of its six
little legs, to play dead. Help me
to like the passionate kiss
of its sting, to do that thing.
Help me to love the wasp.

Moth

A moth is a butterfly's dark twin
dressed in drab wings.
She isn't scary.
Think of her as a different thing –
a plain-clothes fairy.

She loves the electric light
that shines through the window,
just like guess-who
when she's flying in from the garden.
Yes, you!

The moth doesn't bite
or scratch or sting.
She can only hurt herself –
flying too close to the light,
burning her wings.

A Stick Insect's Funeral Poem

co-written with Ella Duffy

Goodbye, Courgette,
insect pet.
You are old and cold.

Goodbye, Courgette,
I won't forget
how tickly you were to hold.

Goodbye, Courgette,
the best pet.
I love you so, like gold.

Oh, Courgette!

The Birds, the Fish and the Insects

1 THE BIRDS

Which is the most communicative of the birds?

Is it the Blackbird?

No, for the Blackbird is the most nosey of the birds.

Is it the Wren?

No, for the Wren is the most architectural of the birds.

Then it is the Coot?

No, for the Coot is the most camp of the birds.

Then it is the Chaffinch?

No, for the Chaffinch is the most pedantic of the birds.

Perhaps it is the Kingfisher?

No, for the Kingfisher is the most passionate of the birds.

Perhaps it is the Magpie?

No, for the Magpie is the most morbid of the birds.

Is it the Nightingale?

No, for the Nightingale is the most quotable of the birds.

Is it the Swallow?

No, for the Swallow is the most fickle of the birds.

Then it is the Woodpecker?

No, for the Woodpecker is the most exasperated of the birds.

Then is it the Crow?

No, for the Crow is the most superstitious of the birds.

Perhaps it is the Raven?

No, for the Raven is the most deranged of the birds.

Perhaps it is the Sparrow?

No, for the Sparrow is the most frugal of the birds.

Is it the Smew?

No, for the Smew is the most sly of the birds.

Is it the Chough?

No, for the Chough is the most pleased of the birds.

Then it is the Curlew?

No, for the Curlew is the most timely of the birds.

Then is it the Gannet?

No, for the Gannet is the most gastronomic of the birds.

Perhaps it is the Merlin?

No, for the Merlin is the most devious of the birds.

Perhaps it is the Grouse?

No, for the Grouse is the most aristocratic of the birds.

Is it the Tawny Owl?

No, for the Tawny Owl is the most clubbable of the birds.

Is it the Oystercatcher?

No, for the Oystercatcher is the most innovative of the birds.

Then it is the Buff-Bellied Pipit?

No, for the Buff-Bellied Pipit is the most operatic of the birds.

Then it is the Canada Goose?

No, for the Canada Goose is the most curious of the birds.

Perhaps it is the Robin?

No, for the Robin is the most devout of the birds.

Perhaps it is the Bee-Eater?

No, for the Bee-Eater is the most taciturn of the birds.

Is it the Great Tit?

No, for the Great Tit is the most harassed of the birds.

Is it the Great Crested Grebe?

No, for the Great Crested Grebe is the most fatuous of the birds.

Then is it the Goldfinch?

No, for the Goldfinch is the most lonely of the birds.

Then is it the Heron?

No, for the Heron is the most smitten of the birds.

So it is the Cuckoo?

Yes! For the Cuckoo is the bird in the wood who heralds Spring.

2 The Fish

Which is the most affectionate of the fish?

Is it the Carp?

No, for the Carp is the most dissatisfied of the fish.

Is it the Flounder?

No, for the Flounder is the most bewildered of the fish.

Then is it the Roach?

No, for the Roach is the most hedonistic of the fish.

Then is it the Sild?

No, for the Sild is the most dyslexic of the fish.

Perhaps it is the Pollock?

No, for the Pollock is the most vulgar of the fish.

Perhaps it is the Whitebait?

No, for the Whitebait is the most tribal of the fish.

Is it the Chub?

No, for the Chub is the most secure of the fish.

Is it the Plaice?

No, for the Plaice is the most trendy of the fish.

Then is it the Herring?

No, for the Herring is the most misleading of the fish.

Then is it the Barbel?

No, for the Barbel is the most garrulous of the fish.

Perhaps it is the Grunion?

No, for the Grunion is the most lachrymose of the fish.

Perhaps it is the Hake?

No, for the Hake is the most haughty of the fish.

Is it the Tench?

No, for the Tench is the most uptight of the fish.

Is it the Ling?

No, for the Ling is the most solicitous of the fish.

Then is it the Bream?

No, for the Bream is the most imaginative of the fish.

Then is it the Cod?

No, for the Cod is the most divine of the fish.

Perhaps it is the Trout?

No, for the Trout is the most officious of the fish.

Perhaps it is the Mackerel?

No, for the Mackerel is the most gullible of the fish.

Is it the Rudd?

No, for the Rudd is the most insolent of the fish.

Is it the Guppy?

No, for the Guppy is the most materialistic of the fish.

Then is it the Halibut?

No, for the Halibut is the most contradictory of the fish.

Then is it the Sprat?

No, for the Sprat is the most insecure of the fish.

Perhaps it is the Marlin?

No, for the Marlin is the most tricksy of the fish.

Perhaps it is the Haddock?

No, for the Haddock is the most charitable of the fish.

Is it the Salmon?

No, for the Salmon is the most enchanted of the fish.

Is it the Stickleback?

No, for the Stickleback is the most maternal of the fish.

Then is it the Piranha?

No, for the Piranha is the most punitive of the fish.

So it is the Sardine?

Yes! For the Sardine is the fish in the ocean that snuggles.

3 THE INSECTS

Which is the most talented of the insects?

Is it the Wasp?

No, for the Wasp is the most sarcastic of the insects.

Is it the Beetle?

No, for the Beetle is the most famous of the insects.

Then is it the Dragonfly?

No, for the Dragonfly is the most wilful of the insects.

Then is it the Ladybird?

No, for the Ladybird is the most literate of the insects.

Perhaps it is the Ant?

No, for the Ant is the most uncomplaining of the insects.

Perhaps it is the Cockroach?

No, for the Cockroach is the most loyal of the insects.

Is it the Midge?

No, for the Midge is the most political of the insects.

Is it the Fly?

No, for the Fly is the most subversive of the insects.

Then is it the Hornet?

No, for the Hornet is the most coiffured of the insects.

Then is it the Earwig?

No, for the Earwig is the most vicarious of the insects.

Perhaps it is the Mosquito?

No, for the Mosquito is the most vindictive of the insects.

Perhaps it is the Centipede?

No, for the Centipede is the most enumerate of the insects.

Is it the Daddy Longlegs?

No, for the Daddy Longlegs is the most condescending of the insects.

Is it the Firefly?

No, for the Firefly is the most naughty of the insects.

Then is it the Greenfly?

No, for the Greenfly is the most conscientious of the insects.

Then is it the Grasshopper?

No, for the Grasshopper is the most puzzled of the insects.

Perhaps it is the Termite?

No, for the Termite is the most stage-struck of the insects.

Perhaps it is the Louse?

No, for the Louse is the most timorous of the insects.

Is it the Moth?

No, for the Moth is the most insomniac of the insects.

Is it the Butterfly?

No, for the Butterfly is the most unfaithful of the insects.

So it is the Bee!

Yes! For the Bee is the insect in the garden that makes honey.

Tight

Henry VIII was tight on his six wives.
Fairy tales are always tight on wolves.
Pollution is tight on briny ocean waves.

Valentine's Day is tight if you're all alone.
History is tight on Anon.
Le feu de joie was tight on Saint Joan.

November the Fifth was tight on Guy Fawkes.
Swear-boxes are tight on saying f***.
Eating with chopsticks is tight on knives and forks.

Diets are tight on fish, chips and mushy peas.
Colony Collapse Disorder is tight on bees.
9 to 5 is tight on a life of ease.

Fanny Brawne was tight on John Keats.
A windless day is tight on flying kites.
Cats are tight on mice and dogs on cats.

Unrequited love is tight on the heart.
Heavy snow is tight on pavement art.
Polite society is *well* tight on the fart.

Snide

Snide's my word.
I'm the lad for snide.
Tried other words, longer words,
words with Latin roots, with syllables.
Didn't like them. Sighed. Decided
to adhere to snide.
My word. Snide.

Something's not my scene?
It's snide.
My teacher is.
Made me stay inside
for spitting
when I'd just swallowed a fly.
Piano practice is –
I'll never reach Grade V.
My Grandma's kisses. Poetry. The News.
The Drama Club.
Laugh? I nearly died.
That bag they put the dog in
when it's needing dried.
Snide.

The Duke of Edinburgh's Award.
Snide.
That time they blew me offside
when I scored.
Snide.
Being stuck in bed with flu
the day it snowed.
Snide.
Seeing my mother cooking in the nude.
Double snide.

Let me be old and rich and idle,
Emperor of Snide.
When I've snored and sneered my way
through life and, aged one-hundred-odd,
have died,
let stonemasons with chisels
come to my grave
and let them carve it there with pride.
My word.
SNIDE.

Seven Deadly Adjectives

1 SLY

He was sly from birth, slithered out
without so much as a cry, lay in his crib,
slit-eyed, silent, sly.

Sleekit, too, as a toddler, slipped a soother
in his zipped lip twenty-four seven, kept
his nappies dry, sly;

slid about as a boy, listening, hearing
no good of himself, hung upside down
in his room like a bat, planning

his tit for tat, his take that; glid downstairs
in his stockinged feet, slipped from the house
like steam, teenaged, a sly moustache

under his nose. He liked being sly, loved it,
courted a sly girl, tall and slim, married her.
Sly twins came.

2 ARGUMENTATIVE

She'd argue black was white
to be right, that blue was red
to say the last word to be said,
that yellow was green, a king
was really a queen, that bright day
was night.

        She'd have it that
the long was the short of it,
the bottom line was only the tip
of the iceberg and fire was ice, insist
that the hill of a mole in the grass
was a mountain, the spill from a hole

in a glass was a fountain. She'd say
home was away, in out, truth doubt,
reason was madness, goodness badness,
argue the toss till heads were tails, peanuts
were huge rocks, small fry were giant whales
in the churning, quarrelling sea.

3 SELFISH

He stashed his sweets in his sock drawer.
He hid his crisps in a bag on a hook on the wall.
He thought to himself – *Self's*
eating them all.

He kept his cakes in his satchel.
He locked crème brûlée in a box in a hole in the floor.
He promised himself – *Self's*
having some more!

He tucked his tuck in his cupboard.
He slid ice-cream behind books no one read on his shelf.
He smiled to himself – *Self's*
seeing to self.

He shut himself in his bedroom.
He got it all out, far away from everyone else.
It was spoiled, alas – exactly
like he was himself, himself, himself.

4 Moody

Those twins were moody, kept themselves
to themselves, hung out in the woods,
their faces sullen, their voices silent,
their hands muddy.

           They sat
at the back of the class at the same desk,
scowled at a shared book, sulked
when they stood up to read, mumbled,

sucked their milk through straws slowly
in a corner of the playground. They liked
the red-haired laughing boy with the ball,
followed him
           at a distance as he bounced
and kicked his way home. Those twins
carried on to the woods, stayed there till dusk,
not talking, digging their big hole.

5 TWO-FACED

Two-faced, two-faced,
she had four eyes.
Two were brown under a black frown,
two were summery skies.

Two-faced, two-faced,
she'd a brace of noses.
One sniffed something fishy,
one roses.

Two-faced, two-faced,
she'd a double chin –
one fat,
t'other thin.

Two-faced, two-faced,
she had four ears.
Two heard only the boos of the crowd,
two heard the cheers.

Two-faced, two-faced,
she had four lips,
between their grins and grimaces
her forked-tongue slipped.

Two-faced, two-faced,
one face never slept,
one face snored in the darkness,
one face forever wept.

6 BOASTFUL

He'd boast
he was best
if he played Beast
to Beauty.

He'd brag
in a brogue
he was Big
like it was a duty.

He'd bluff
till belief
floated off
like a pink balloon.

He'd strut
down the street
heading straight
for a fall – and soon.

7 LAZY

She had lazy, lazy bones.
She had stones in the shoes on her feet.
She had lazy, lazy, lazy bones.
She ignored the people she'd meet.

She had lazy, lazy blood.
She had mud in the nails of her hand.
She had lazy, lazy, lazy blood.
She never had anything planned.

She had lazy, lazy skin.
She had gums but no teeth in her grin.
She had lazy, lazy, lazy skin.
She wouldn't let anyone in.

She had lazy, lazy bones.
She slept under a blanket of earth.
O lazy, lazy, lazy bones,
how does death differ from birth?

Fine Weather

The dead like fine weather, their cold bones
grow warm in the soil, under the daffodils,
the tulips, the roses, under the heather.

The dead enjoy sunshine, their pale skulls
are new-laid eggs in the ground, their coffins
brown as toast. The dead love summer most –

when the living come, in dresses or shirt-sleeves,
to picnic by their graves. The dead relax, bask,
as sunlight heals their stones, their dates, their names.

Little Ghost

Think of me as a child
who has swallowed herself whole –
gulp, gone –
leaving only
the colour of goat's cheese,
the hue of a buried bone,
the tint of the last dab of vanilla ice-cream
in a cone.

I'm all alone
in the Library
with the old books;
have been for ages.
My smoky fingers can't turn the pages.
I'm so-o-o bored.
I make a portrait fall
from the wall
to the floor – CRASH –
in one of my sudden rages.
Scary. Spooky. Totally freaky.
I pipe my thin spirit noise
on the limy-lemony air.
Oooooooooo. Creepy.

I'm not here, not there,
untouched, unheard, unseen.
Think of me as a film
escaped from a screen,
a has-been,
an absolute scream.

Think of me as a late guest,
a gust of wind,
dancing dust on the air.
What is my name? Can you guess?
Do you know, you foolish scared creature?
My name is Little Ghost.

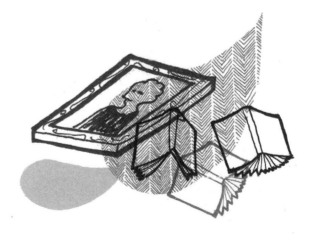

Touched

A ghost touched me. Elizabeth Norris. Don't laugh.
It's true; her hand on my cheek, cool as a flannel
dropped in a drained bath.

                      Felt by a ghost, me;
don't grin. I nearly screamed – chill fingers
under my chin, a sister of ice, she,
coaxing me in,

              in, to the cold space
of her past. I gasped as she read my lips
with her fingertips, Tudor, dead, laid her head
on my shoulder

              like a sad friend. Poor Elizabeth,
she touched me, here, in my heart – for how, now,
though we never met, could we ever part?

Don't Be Scared

The dark is only a blanket
for the moon to put on her bed.

The dark is a private cinema
for the movie dreams in your head.

The dark is a little black dress
to show off the sequin stars.

The dark is the wooden hole
behind the strings of happy guitars.

The dark is a jeweller's velvet cloth
where children sleep like pearls.

The dark is a spool of film
to photograph boys and girls,

so smile in your sleep in the dark.
Don't be scared.

Boo! to a Goose

She wouldn't say *Boo!* to a goose.
But she played cards with a puss
and gambled her dosh.

She wouldn't say *Boo!* to a goose.
But she went out to dine with a grouse
at the Hotel de Posh.

She wouldn't say *Boo!* to a goose.
But she danced all night with a moose
by the light of the moon.

She wouldn't say *Boo!* to a goose.
But she supped with a couple of newts
from a golden spoon.

She wouldn't say *Boo!* to a goose.
But she rode on the back of a mouse
in a field of corn.

She wouldn't say *Boo!* to a goose.
But she haunted a house with a ghost
from dusk till dawn.

But she wouldn't say *Boo!*
She wouldn't say *Boo!*
She wouldn't say *Boo!* to a goose.

Be Very Afraid

of the Spotted Pyjama Spider
which disguises itself as a spot
on the sleeve of your nightwear,
waits till you fall asleep,
then commences its ominous creep
towards your face.

        Be very afraid
of the Hanging Lightcord Snake
which waits in the dark
for your hand to reach for the switch,
then wraps itself round your wrist
with a venomous hiss. Be afraid,

very afraid, of the Toothpaste Worm
which is camouflaged as a stripe of red
in the paste you squeeze
and oozes onto your brush
with a wormy guile
to squirm on your smile.

Be very afraid indeed
of the Bookworm Bat
which wraps itself like a dust-jacket
over a book,
then flaps and squeaks in your face
when you take a look. Be afraid

of the Hairbrush Rat, of the Merit Badge Beetle,
of the Bubble Bath Jellyfish
and the Wrist Watch Tick (with its terrible nip),
of the Sock Wasp, of the Bee in the Bonnet
(posed as an amber jewel
in the hatpin on it). Be feart

of the Toilet Roll Scorpion,
snug as a bug in its cardboard tube
until someone disturbs it,
of the Killer Earring Ant,
dangling from a lobe
until someone perturbs it. Don't be brave –

be very afraid.

Quicksand

Mrs Leather's told you about quicksand;
now you're scared.
You'd take the short-cut through the muddy field
if you dared.

But quicksand takes a laced-up shoe,
a white sock,
then sips a trembling pair of knees.
Its moist suck

drinks the hem of a new blue dress
to the waist.
Your hands will panic over your head,
claw at space.

Quicksand under your armpits, up to your chin.
Now you drown
the way Mrs Leather said you would.
The whole town

comes searching, searching with blankets and lights.
But too late –
only your satchel's found, at dawn, at the edge of the field
by this gate.

A Worry

It's come to live in my room – a worry.
I asked when was it planning to leave?
It said it was in no particular hurry.
It's not slimy and it's not furry.
It's not clammy and it's not hairy.
I can't describe it.
When I whip round to stare it straight
in the eye, it's not there.
But believe me,
if there's one thing I know for certain, for sure,
I know that the worry's there.

It hunkers down. It squats.
Its breathing swaps the colour of my room
from cheerful to gloom. The curtains look drawn.
The bed is a wreck.
My face in the mirror looks like a vampire's had a takeaway
from the neck.
It's there at dawn – the worry.
I've told it I'm too young to marry!
I want to be free!
No no no no no, it said,
I belong to it forever and it belongs to me.

Help! Au secours! Mayday!
What can I do?
Will anyone credit the size the worry has grown to?
A rat. A mongrel. A puma. An ape. A creature from Mars.
Can anyone hear the sound of the worry's voice?
A wasp. Slow handclaps. A dentist's drill. The squealing brakes
of skidding cars.
And what about other girls?
What about boys?
Do they have worry growing like fungi
over their books and toys?

Now life is hell.
Life is a horrid trick.
I'm worried sick.

Whirlpool

I saw two hands in the whirlpool
clutching at air,
but when I knelt by the swirling edge
nothing was there.
Behind me, twelve tall green-black trees shook
and scattered their rooks.
I turned to the spinning waters again
and looked.

I saw two legs in the whirlpool
dancing deep.
I see that horrible choreography still
in my turning sleep.
Then I heard the dog from Field o' Blood Farm
howl on its chain;
and gargling out from the whirlpool came the watery sound
of a name.

I bent my head to the whirlpool,
I saw a face,
Then I knew that I should run for my life
away from that place.
But my eyes and mouth were opening wide, far below
as I drowned.
And the words I tell were silver fish
the day I was found.

Tales of the Expected

1 THE MONSTER OF GHOSTY BOG

When a sudden mist swirled in from the sea
to muffle and blindfold the town,
those who were out – and I was one –
hurried for home, hoods up, heads down.

Legend claimed that the Monster of Ghosty Bog
would prowl through the salty fog, ravenous,
in search of a kid to bite and gobble and chew.
The townsfolk would find a little bone next day,

a sock or a shoe, a muddy toy . . . no girl or boy
was safe when the mist boiled in from the waves
to poach the wriggling town. The Monster would pin
you down! The Monster would suck your eyes

like boiled sweets! The Monster would leave your brains
on the side of the street! Beware! Take care!
Parents who let their child play out would soon come
to grieve it. So legend had it. But no one believed it.

2 Ghoul School

The Headmaster isn't a vampire.
He doesn't drink blood,
or sleep in a coffiny bed
with a duvet of mud.

The Deputy Head's no werewolf.
She doesn't noisily eat
the Infants for hors d'oeuvres
and the Juniors for sweet.

The teachers aren't ghouls.
Their yellow teeth don't bite
the trembling hands of pupils
learning to read and write.

The school isn't a ghost ship
floating away from the town . . .
nobody left on board . . .
a bell ringing for the drowned.

3 The Dark

If you think of the dark
as a black park
and the moon as a bounced ball,
then there's nothing to be frightened of
at all.

(Except for aliens . . .)

The Childminders

I was six when I went to see
if a brace of childminders
would suit small me.

They lived where the sun
couldn't quite reach.
A corner house. Number 101.

One childminder was tall, stooped, thin,
and three or four teeth
short of a grin.

Childminder Two was of smaller build,
with boiled red eyes.
My blood chilled.

They had one toy. They had one book.
They said: *Here, little girl,*
have a good look.

The toy was a broken clockwork mouse.
The book was as dusty
as the gloomy house.

I'm afraid I won't require you, I smiled
and backed away. Then I saw,
to my horror, a skeletal child –

slumped in the corner, bored to death.
There but for the grace of god . . .
I thought, and left.

The Babysitter

Once upon a time, nearly fifty years ago,
when people sent a letter they wrote
Postman, Don't Be Slow,
Be like Elvis, Go Man Go, on the envelopes
and a sparky little girl called Bobbie B. May
prayed for a miracle day after day. This was it:
Please send Elvis to babysit.

Elvis looked like a prince. He played the guitar.
He had a happy white smile. He had blue-black hair.
He sang rock'n'roll. He sang the blues.
He didn't want anyone to step on his blue suede shoes.

Every Saturday night round about six
the snitch on the latch on the gate would click.
Bobbie B. May would run downstairs,
fling open the front door . . .
but the answer to her prayers was sneezy Mrs Blueberry
(who always wore a hat)
or gentle Miss Grass
(who lived alone with her cat)
or Grandma and Grampa or bean-pole Uncle Leslie.
No good!
Bobbie B. May wanted Elvis Presley.

Night after night Bobbie B. would stare
at the blue suede sky with its far bright star.
I have one prayer. This is it.
Please send Elvis to babysit.

The year rolled on. One Saturday near Christmas
Bobbie B. was waiting for the babysitter.
She looked out of the window.
There in the snow
was a pink Cadillac!
With a peak-capped driver!
And Elvis in the back!
He wore a white drape jacket and spangly gold jeans.
He was offering the driver a jelly bean.

Bobbie B. ran outside in her two bare feet. *Elvis!*
Have you come to babysit?
Elvis gave a smile, lopsided, shy.
I guess I have, Miss Bobbie. Can I bring my guitar?
Shall we go inside?
Bobbie B. May
almost
died!

Elvis sat down by the Christmas tree,
he strummed his guitar,
he winked at Bobbie B.
Then he started to sing *Good Rockin' Tonight.*
His gold jeans sparkled in the Christmas lights.
Have you heard the news? Everybody's rockin' tonight.
Have you heard the news? Everybody's rockin' tonight.
Bobbie B. danced around the living-room.
High in the sky was a yellow moon
like a gold LP.
Elvis Presley's babysitting ME! thought Bobbie.

Nearly fifty years ago
when Elvis was King
Bobbie B. May heard him sing.
He sang in the kitchen as she ate ice cream.
He sang in the bathroom as she brushed her teeth.
You Ain't Nothin' But A Hound Dog he sang on the stairs
and *Lawdy Miss Clawdy* as she combed her hair.
But best of all, as the evening ended,
was *Love Me Tender* sung slow and deep
as Bobbie B. May
fell
fast
asleep.

Against the midnight sky a shooting star
slashed like a hand on the strings of a guitar.
When Bobbie woke up
Elvis was gone.
She walked in his foot prints in the firm white snow,
she wandered round the house where he'd sung his songs.
But on Christmas morning by the tinselly tree
were a little pair of blue suede shoes
addressed
to Bobbie B.

Beebop Da Beebop

A woman in Stafford said
I'm going to the market to shop,
at the same time as a woman in Paris said
This endless rain will not stop,

at the same time as a girl in Halifax said
He kissed me full on the lips,
at the same time as a woman in Istanbul said
I need a replacement hip,

at the same time as a woman in Oslo said
May I purchase a pound of pork chops?
at the same time as a man in Edinburgh said
I name this ship . . .

at the same time as a man in New York said
I'm into hip hop!
at the same time as a girl in Amsterdam said
The canals are so deep,

at the same time as a boy in Nottingham said
Spiders give me the creeps,
at the same time as a woman in Montreal said
That aeroplane's looping the loop!

at the same time as a girl in Exeter said
The baby's asleep,
at the same time as a man in Jerusalem said
I'm King of the heap!

at the same time as a woman in Cardiff said
Who won the Cup?
at the same time as a girl in Antwerp said
Can I sit on your lap?

at the same time as a boy in Tranmere said
Our team hasn't a hope,
at the same time as a man in Dallas said
It's all a load of hype,

at the same time as a man in London said
It's a definite nope,
at the same time as a man in Madrid said
What colour's the strip?

at the same time as a woman in Berlin said
He eats like an ape!
at the same time as a boy in Venice said
Don't be a dope!

at the same time as a man in Bali said
Do you fancy a grape?
at the same time as a woman in Sydney said
I was the dupe,

at the same time as a man in Memphis said
Beebop da beebop, beebop da beebop,
at the same time as a girl in Manchester said
Beebop da beebop, beebop da beebop.

The Manchester Cows

1 Arrival

Cows arrived.
Clouds stopped raining.
Crowds of people
stopped complaining.

2 Harvey Nicks

A girl called
Annabel Jessica Pickles
bumped into a cow
in Harvey Nichols.

3 Chinatown

A gentle cow
in Chinatown
ate steamed har kau,
washed it down
with jasmine tea,
then for pudding
had lychee.

4 SCHOOL

At Manchester High School for Cows,
the favourite lesson is Mooing –
they all make a terrible row,
then it's off down to lunch for some Chewing.

5 SHOPPING

The cow in Oilily was silly.
The cow in Jigsaw was RUDE.
In Daisy and Tom, the cow sang a song
(or tried to – it really just mooed).

6 COLOURS

A red cow
stands in goal
at Old Trafford.

Outside the City Art Gallery
a creamy cubist cow
dreams of Picasso.

A yellow cow
ambles down the Curry Mile
under a harvest moon.

The pink cow
in Didsbury Village
is GORGEOUS –
and knows it.

The sad blue cow
stands in the Southern Cemetery rain
till love, till love,
returns again.

7 CREATURES

Six silly cows
on a hen night
at a zebra crossing.

8 HAIKOW

Moo moo moo moo moo,
Moo moo moo moo moo moo moo,
Moo moo moo moo moo.

9 GREAT COW ARTISTS

PICOWSSO

MOONET

MICHELANGELOW

CONSTABLE

MOODIGLIANI

MOOTISSE

LEONARDO BAA VINCI (he was a sheep, actually)

EDVARD MOONCH (his most famous painting is
The Cream)

OSCAR COWKOSCHKA

EL GRECOW

FRIDA COWLO

10 BEST FRIEND

If my best friend was a cow,
her hide would feel like silk,
and she'd be full of lemonade,
not milk.

      Her udders would be bagpipes,
they'd play a Scottish tune,
and we'd dance together,
two daft cows,
then jump right over the moon.

11 HOTEL

Two cows swanned into
the Midland Hotel,
all dressed up
and wearing bells;
had tea and toast –
'what fun!' they said –
then took the lift
and went to bed.

The Great Bed of Ware

The night I kipped in the Great Bed of Ware,
there were
        eleven
            other
                sleepers there;
twenty-four feet, including mine,
at the foot of the bed
           in a
              stinky
                  line.
Did we snore?
Did we care!
Sleeping and snoozing in the Great Bed of Ware.

The night I dossed in the Great Bed of Ware
there was a butcher,
           a baker,
                a candlestick-maker,
a spy, a nun, a guitar-man,
a teacher and a preacher,
a brain-surgeon,
          a puppy,
              a juggler
                  and a millionaire.
Some wore pyjamas,
one wore fur,
dreaming and dribbling in the Great Bed of Ware.

The night I crashed in the Great Bed of Ware
one of we twelve
                          had a bad
                                         nightmare.
One ground her teeth,
                          one wet the bed,
one had a nightcap on his head,
seven snuggled up
                          while an eighth one read
a bedtime story,
then we all went Z.

The night I flopped in the Great Bed of Ware,
the nun knelt down
                          and said a prayer,
the teacher
              and the preacher
                                      and the guitar-man
all joined in on the last *Amen,*
the butcher and the baker
                              had a pillow-fight,
till the candlestick-maker
                                snuffed out the light,
the juggler juggled
                          in the gathering dark,
the little puppy began to bark
so the millionaire sang a lullaby . . .
lulla lee, lulla loo,
lulla lare, lulla lie . . .
How do I know this?
                          I was there –
I was the spy
                  in the Great Bed of Ware!

Song

As I walked in a garden green
I heard a singing girl,
her song a sure and silver line
which pulled me from the world
to where she sat, the flowers wild,
crooning to a little child –
Lull, lully, lully, lulla lay,
all words are living flesh today,
lull, lully, lalla lay.

I sat down underneath a tree.
For thirty years I'd walked
dragging my shadow after me
and never heard it talk,
but now it sighed upon the grass –
a child, a girl, is born today
and she is yours to take away,
lull, lully lully, lulla lay,
lull, lully, lalla lay.

My shadow turned into a babe.
I turned into a girl.
The song I sang was new to me,
yet I knew every word
and rocked the infant in my arms,
keeping her from harm.
Lull, lully, lully, lulla lay,
all words are living flesh today,
lull, lully, lalla lay.

The Song Collector

The first song I gathered was that of a man locked up
in a cell, who sang to the mournful toll of the prison bell
as I walked by: *This morning I'm going to die, to die,*
and only the girl who loved me once knows why.

The second song was sung by a lad in a lane
where I swayed on a stile, swigging my ale,
so I asked him to sing it again for a coin and he did:
This is simply the simple song of a simple kid.

Song three was trilled by a bunch of nuns – that
was a Latin one, *dominus, dominum* – outside a church,
and four, five, six, I picked from a farm, eye-high
in corn, as I chanced my tattooed arm at harvesting.

Stopped counting then, when I got to ten, and the next
I knew I had more than a few to my repertoire;
so I bought a guitar, played four to the bar, wandered
wide and far, with an ear for a humming lad or a yodelling girl.

With an ear for a whistling train, for a foghorn ship.
With an ear for percussion rain, for the tune the wind blows
through the trees. With an ear for the birds and bees,
yippees, for quavers, crotchets, minims, doh ray me's.

Johann Sebastian Baa

Johann Sebastian Baa
was a very talented sheep.
He could write the most sublime music
in his sleep.

All the other animals
would crowd around
to listen to the divine mathematics
of his sheepish sound.

Then Johann Sebastian Baa
played his latest piece,
a genius from the tip of his hoof
to the end of his fleece.

Johann Sebastian Baa
knew the score.
The pigs and cows and donkeys
shouted *More! More! More!*

His Nine Sympathies

were for the mothers,
listening to flute scales stop and start;

and for the fathers,
whistling their tired ways home in the dark;

for younger brothers,
sent with the jingling cows to market;

or for eldest daughters,
hymned up the aisles till death did them part;

for orphans,
led by a piper out of a pretty park;

and for paupers,
scraping their fiddles for small change in a hat;

for old ones,
tapping their sticks on the twisting path;

for soldiers,
stamping their boots on a victory march;

and for the lovers,
the broken chords of their hearts.

A Child's Song

Earth, earth, under my shoe,
you will swallow me whole.
I know you, earth,
you've a quicksand soul.

Sky, sky, over my hat,
you will fall on my head.
I know what you're up to, sky,
you'll flatten me dead.

Sea, sea, inside my socks,
you will drink me in.
I know not to trust you, sea,
you've a shark's grin.

Wind, wind, under my coat,
you will snuff me out.
I know your game, wind,
your hand's at my throat.

World, world, outside my room,
you will close your eye
till everything's dark and black
as the day I'll die.

Spell

A clip of thinder ever the reeftips
sends like a bimb going iff!
My hurt thimps in my chist.

It's dirk. The clods are block with reen.
The wand blues in the trays.
There's no mean.

I smuggle ender my blinkets
and coddle my toddy.
Sloop will have drums in it.

Teacher

When you teach me,
your hands bless the air
where chalk dust sparkles.

And when you talk,
the six wives of Henry VIII
stand in the room like bridesmaids,

or the Nile drifts past the classroom window,
the Pyramids baking like giant cakes
on the playing fields.

You teach with your voice,
so a tiger prowls from a poem
and pads between desks, black and gold

in the shadow and sunlight,
or the golden apples of the sun drop
from a branch in my mind's eye.

I bow my head again
to this tattered, doodled book
and learn what love is.

Mrs Hamilton's Register

Grace and beauty?
Annie, here.
Eternal blossom?
Amarachi, here.
Celestial spirit?
Devashree, here.
One to admire?
Emily, here.
Light of a girl?
Ella, here.
Heaven's benevolence?
Gianina, here.
Hill near meadows?
Georgina, here.
Kind angel?
Juanaya, here.
Sea of riches?
Molly, here.
Victorious heart?
Nicola, here.
Little one?
Polly, here.
Lovely flower?
Rosie, here.
Twilight hour?
Sharvari, here.
Soft dark eyes?
Siya, here.
Thank you, girls.
Thank you, Mrs Hamilton.

The Laugh of Your Class

Your class laughs like fourteen birds
in a tree.
Your class laughs like ice in a glass
on a tray.
Your class laughs like the stars
in the Milky Way.
Ha ha ha ha ha ho ho hee hee.

Your class laughs like the horn
of a bright red car.
Your class laughs like the strings
on a loud guitar.
Your class laughs like the harmony
of a choir.
Ho ho ho ho ho hee hee ha ha.

Your class laughs like the hiss
of skis on snow.
Your class laughs like the screams
at a circus show.
Your class laughs like a trumpet player's
blow.
Hee hee hee hee hee ha ha ho ho.

Your class laughs like fourteen seals
in the sea.
Your class laughs like a drunken
chimpanzee.
Your class laughs like the buzz
of a honey bee.
Ha ha ha ha ha ho ho hee hee.

Your class laughs like the mighty
ocean's roar.
Your class laughs like carol singers
at the door.
Your class laughs like an elephant
in the shower.
Ho ho ho ho ho hee hee ha ha.

Your class laughs like doh ray me
fa so.
Your class laughs like seven dwarves singing
hi ho.
Your class laughs like blue whales
when they blow.
Hee hee hee hee hee ha ha ho ho.
Ha ha ha ha ha ho ho hee hee.
Ho ho ho ho ho hee hee ha ha.
Hee hee hee hee hee ha ha ho ho.

I Adore Year 3

I went past their door.
I went past their door.
They were asleep on the floor!
Year 4.

I went past their door.
I went past their door.
I heard them all snore!
Year 4.

I went past their door.
I went past their door.
It must be a bore!
Year 4.

I went past their door.
I went past their door.
I want to ignore
Year 4.

I went past their door.
I went past their door.
The future I saw!
Year 4.

Year 3 I adore!
Year 3! I want more –
Till I go through the door
Till I (Aaagh!) go through the door
Till I go (No! No!) through the door
of Year 4.

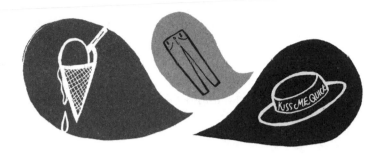

The Alphabest

Aye! to avocados stuffed with prawns.

Bravo! to bowling on smooth green lawns.

Cool! to Christmas and Santa Claus.

Delightful! to dogs who extend their paws.

Encore! to everyone who takes the stage.

Fab! to the fairy on the storybook page.

Gorgeous! to the girl in designer jeans.

Hurrah! to the heir of the reigning queen.

I likey! to the ice cream dripping down my cone.

Jolly good! to the jacket on my mobile phone.

Kiss! to the kid with the Kiss-Me-Quick hat.

Lovely! to the lady with the sleek black cat.

Marvellous! to minestrone with bread to dip.

Nice one! to the number on the winning slip.

OK! to the owner of a brand new car.

Perfect! to the pop star with the loud guitar.

Quintessential! to the queue for a bestselling book.

Respect! to the rapper with the coolest look.

Smashing! to sextuplets on a mother's knee.

Tops! to the thrush singing in the tree.

Up! with umbrellas in springtime rain.

Vote! for Vegetarians Against Animal Pain.

Wicked! to waffles with chocolate sauce.

Xcellent! to XXX (means I love you, of course).

Yes! to the yellow of a soft-boiled egg.

Zooper-dooper! to the zoo with the dinosaur egg.

Your School

Your school knows the names of places –
Dhaka, Rajshahi, Sylket, Khulna, Chittagong –
and where they are.
Your school knows where rivers rise –
the Ganges, Brahmaputra, Thames –
and knows which seas they join.
Your school knows the height of mountains
disappearing into cloud.

Your school knows important dates,
the days when history turned around
to stare the human race
straight in the face.
Your school knows the poets' names, long dead –
John Keats, Rabindranath Tagore, Sylvia Plath –
and what they said.
It knows the paintings hanging in the old gold frames
in huge museums
and how the artists lived and loved
who dipped their brushes in the vivid paint.

Your school knows the language of the world –
hello, namaskar, sat sri akal, as-salaam-o-aleykum, salut –
it knows the homes of faith,
the certainties of science,
the living art of sport.
Your school knows what Isaac Newton thought,
what William Shakespeare wrote
and what Mohammed taught.

Your school knows your name –
Shirin, Abdul, Aysha, Rayhan, Lauren, Jack –
and who you are.
Your school knows the most important thing to know –
you are a star,
a star.

The Fruits, the Vegetables, the Flowers and the Trees

1 THE FRUITS

Which is the most friendly of the fruits?

Is it the apple?

No, for the apple is the most romantic of the fruits.

Is it the apricot?

No, for the apricot is the most self-conscious of the fruits.

Then is it the cherry?

No, for the cherry is the most cheerful of the fruits.

Then is it the raspberry?

No, for the raspberry is the most rude of the fruits.

Perhaps it is the quince?

No, for the quince is the most ironic of the fruits.

Perhaps it is the grape?

No, for the grape is the most healing of the fruits.

Is it the damson?

No, for the damson is the most particular of the fruits.

Is it the fig?

No, for the fig is the most demure of the fruits.

Then is it the Victoria plum?

No, for the Victoria plum is the most solemn of the fruits.

Then is it the kumquat?

No, for the kumquat is the most clever of the fruits.

Perhaps it is the pineapple?

No, for the pineapple is the most spiteful of the fruits.

Perhaps it is the lemon?

No, for the lemon is the most naive of the fruits.

Is it the melon?

No, for the melon is the most optimistic of the fruits.

Is it the orange?

No, for the orange is the most gregarious of the fruits.

Then is it the ugli fruit?

No, for the ugli fruit is the most intellectual of the fruits.

Then is it the tangerine?

No, for the tangerine is the most festive of the fruits.

Perhaps it is the elderberry?

No, for the elderberry is the most fussy of the fruits.

Perhaps it is the nectarine?

No, for the nectarine is the most sartorial of the fruits.

Is it the juniper berry?

No, for the juniper berry is the most cunning of the fruits.

Is it the watermelon?

No, for the watermelon is the most extrovert of the fruits.

Then is it the pomegranate?

No, for the pomegranate is the most macabre of the fruits.

Then is it the star fruit?

No, for the star fruit is the most wilful of the fruits.

Perhaps it is the date?

No, for the date is the most punctual of the fruits.

Perhaps it is the coconut?

No, for the coconut is the most lenient of the fruits.

Is it the lychee?

No, for the lychee is the most flirtatious of the fruits.

Is it the gooseberry?

No, for the gooseberry is the most intrusive of the fruits.

Then is it the mandarin?

No, for the mandarin is the most feudal of the fruits.

Then is it the kiwi fruit?

No, for the kiwi fruit is the most poetic of the fruits.

So it is the banana!

Yes! For the banana is the fruit in the bowl that smiles.

2 THE VEGETABLES

Which is the most intelligent of the vegetables?

Is it asparagus?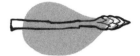

No, for asparagus is the most aloof of the vegetables.

Is it green beans?

No, for green beans are the most parochial of the vegetables.

Then is it carrots?

No, for carrots are the most perceptive of the vegetables.

Then is it dill?

No, for dill is the most confused of the vegetables.

Perhaps it is kale?

No, for kale is the most derivative of the vegetables.

Perhaps it is lettuce?

No, for lettuce is the most sluggish of the vegetables.

Is it broccoli?

No, for broccoli is the most bored of the vegetables.

Is it haricot beans?

No, for haricot beans are the most pretentious of the vegetables.

Then is it iceberg lettuce?

No, for iceberg lettuce is the most trivial of the vegetables.

Then is it onions?

No, for onions are the most attention-seeking of the vegetables.

Perhaps it is spinach?

No, for spinach is the most relaxed of the vegetables.

Perhaps it is endive?

No, for endive is the most over-dressed of the vegetables.

Is it mangetout?

No, for mangetout is the most bossy of the vegetables.

Is it turnip?

No, for turnip is the most spooky of the vegetables.

Then is it Jerusalem artichokes?

No, for Jerusalem artichokes are the most stubborn of the vegetables.

Then is it peas?

No, for peas are the most polite of the vegetables.

Perhaps it is fennel?

No, for fennel is the most bohemian of the vegetables.

Perhaps it is rocket?

No, for rocket is the most effete of the vegetables.

Is it watercress?

No, for watercress is the most ornamental of the vegetables.

Is it new potatoes?

No, for new potatoes are the most childish of the vegetables.

Then is it zucchini?

No, for zucchini are the most bilingual of the vegetables.

Then is it yam?

No, for yam is the most calm of the vegetables.

So it is the cauliflower!

Yes! For the cauliflower is the vegetable in the rack with a brain.

3 THE FLOWERS

Which is the most besotted of the flowers?

Is it the buttercup?

No, for the buttercup is the most nostalgic of the flowers.

Is it the daffodil?

No, for the daffodil is the most literary of the flowers.

Then is it the poppy?

No, for the poppy is the most bereaved of the flowers.

Then is it jasmine?

No, for jasmine is the most sophisticated of the flowers.

Perhaps it is the lily?

No, for the lily is the most ceremonial of the flowers.

Perhaps it is the fuchsia?

No, for the fuchsia is the most expectant of the flowers.

Is it the anemone?

No, for the anemone is the most paranoid of the flowers.

Is it the orchid?

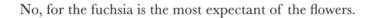

No, for the orchid is the most heartbroken of the flowers.

Then is it the tulip?

No, for the tulip is the most artistic of the flowers.

Then is it the snapdragon?

No, for the snapdragon is the most hospitable of the flowers.

Perhaps it is the lupin?

No, for the lupin is the most vigilant of the flowers.

Perhaps it is the crocus?

No, for the crocus is the most reliable of the flowers.

Is it the thistle?

No, for the thistle is the most patriotic of the flowers.

Is it the hollyhock?

No, for the hollyhock is the most homesick of the flowers.

Then is it the chrysanthemum?

No, for the chrysanthemum is the most pompous of the flowers.

Then is it the violet?

No, for the violet is the most devoted of the flowers.

Perhaps it is gladioli?

No, for gladioli are the most pleased of the flowers.

Perhaps it is the foxglove?

No, for the foxglove is the most dexterous of the flowers.

Is it japonica?

No, for japonica is the most meditative of the flowers.

Is it the iris?

No, for the iris is the most watchful of the flowers.

Then is it the wallflower?

No, for the wallflower is the most hopeful of the flowers.

Then is it the snowdrop?

No, for the snowdrop is the most truthful of the flowers.

Perhaps it is the marigold?

No, for the marigold is the most confident of the flowers.

Perhaps it is the petunia?

No, for the petunia is the most timid of the flowers.

Is it the geranium?

No, for the geranium is the most predictable of the flowers.

Is it the daisy?

No, for the daisy is the most sociable of the flowers.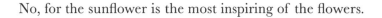

Then is it the sunflower?

No, for the sunflower is the most inspiring of the flowers.

So it is the rose!

Yes! For the rose is the flower in the garden of love.

4 THE TREES

Which is the most hilarious of the trees?

Is it the oak?

No, for the oak is the most loyal of the trees.

Is it the weeping willow?

No, for the weeping willow is the most sensitive of the trees.

Then is it the poplar?

No, for the poplar is the most gossipy of the trees.

Then is it the silver birch?

No, for the silver birch is the most magical of the trees.

Perhaps it is the horse chestnut?

No, for the horse chestnut is the most playful of the trees.

Perhaps it is the ash?

No, for the ash is the most addictive of the trees.

Is it the elm?

No, for the elm is the most quizzical of the trees.

Is it the fir?

No, for the fir is the most jovial of the trees.

Then is it the yew?

No, for the yew is the most vocational of the trees.

Then is it the larch?

No, for the larch is the most kind of the trees.

Perhaps it is the Judas tree?

No, for the Judas tree is the most unreliable of the trees.

Perhaps it is the beech?

No, for the beech is the most zany of the trees.

Is it the palm tree?

No, for the palm tree is the most protective of the trees.

Is it the rowan?

No, for the rowan is the most querulous of the trees.

Then is it the ginkgo?

No, for the ginkgo is the most superior of the trees.

Perhaps it is the Douglas fir?

No, for the Douglas fir is the most clannish of the trees.

Perhaps it is the elder?

No, for the elder is the most experienced of the trees.

Is it the iroko?

No, for the iroko is the most fearless of the trees.

Is it the cedar?

No, for the cedar is the most grandiose of the trees.

Then is it the handkerchief tree?

No, for the handkerchief tree is the most solicitous of the trees.

Then is it the teak?

No, for the teak is the most yielding of the trees.

Perhaps it is the little nut tree?

No, for the little nut tree is the most fabulous of the trees.

Perhaps it is the alder?

No, for the alder is the most anecdotal of the trees.

So it is the monkey puzzle tree!

Yes! For the monkey puzzle tree is the funniest tree in the forest.

Cucumbers

Money is cucumbers now.
My mother earns twenty thousand a year.
Cucumbers don't grow on trees, she snaps,
but gives me four of them each week,
two for each deep pocket of my winter coat,
pocket-money.

Folk keep their cucumbers in banks.
Innumerable cucumbers,
cool and green,
in the ice-cold, deep-freeze safes.
Some folk are millionaires,
they own so many.

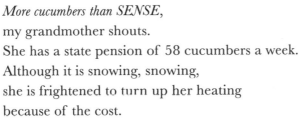

More cucumbers than SENSE,
my grandmother shouts.
She has a state pension of 58 cucumbers a week.
Although it is snowing, snowing,
she is frightened to turn up her heating
because of the cost.

My teacher writes:
On what could you spend one hundred cucumbers?
My mind goes blank.
I stare at the empty page of my exercise book
for a long time
with my shiny, pale-green eyes.

Halo

I was as good as gold, an angel, said ta very much, no thanks,
yes *please*, smiled politely
when I said hello, helped out, tried;
so it came to pass I awoke
and there in the bed
next to my head on the pillow
a halo glowed, a hoop-la of gold.
I didn't faint or scream
or wake up and find it was only a dream,
but went to the mirror
and stared at the icon of me –
acne, bad hair, pyjamas, sticky-out ears, halo.

On the way to school
I swished the halo along with a stick
up the road, down the hill, round the bend
where I frisbeed it to my good friend Dominic Gill,
who caught it, said *What's this then, mate?*
A halo, chum, I'm a saint.
No, you ain't.

Delicate, quaint, the halo settled itself
at the back of my head,
shining and bright,
shedding its numinous light all through Maths,
double English, RK, PE, lunch, History, silent reading.
The teachers stared
but left me alone,
and I kept my eyes on the numbers, the verbs,
the prophets, the dates, the poem,
till the bell rang, then legged it for home.

But some big kids snatched my halo
as I ran through the park;
tossed it between them, kicked it, flicked it,
lobbed it,
far too high for me,
into the outstretched branches of a tree.
Then dusk lapped at my feet
and the navy-blue sea of the sky
floated the moon
as I watched the light of my halo dissolve
to the pinprick glow of a worm,
and heard the loudening shout of a voice
calling, calling my human name.

Numbers

1. 64

Eight 8-year-olds
sat in a tree
swinging their legs.

How high have we climbed? asked one.
What if we fall?
another one said.

Look at the sky!
shrieked a third.
Said the fourth, *Why is it red?*

We're so small,
sobbed a fifth.
And young! wept a sixth.

Said the seventh,
*We're motherless birds
in a nest.*

*But how many years,
how many years are we all?*
sang the one in the yellow dress.

2. Bad Number

70 mice in a pillow case.
70 spots on a greasy face.
70 wasps in a jar of jam.
70 rats in a baby's pram.

70 bones in an open grave.
70 skulls in an empty cave.
70 fleas on a mad stray dog.
70 shoes in a stinking bog.
70 teeth in a vampire's mouth.
70 magpies flying south.

70 nails in a coffin lid.
70 pennies in a quid.
70 grey hairs on a head.
70 children in one bed.
70 eggs in a frying pan.
70 cops in a big black van.
70 prisoners in a cell.
70 rings on a funeral bell.
70 reasons all for NO.
70 arrows in a bow.

70 fake pearls on a neck.
70 sailors in a wreck.
70 holes in a fishing-net.
70 goals in the back of the net.
70 words on a toilet wall.
70 strangers in the hall.
70 wolves at a pig's front door.
70 hours with a world-class bore.
70 kittens in a well.
70 devils down in Hell.

70 cows on an abattoir hook.
70 sums in a homework book.
70 teachers in a row.
70 footprints in the snow
70 nappies in a sink.

70 types of tea to drink.
70 programmes on the telly.
70 chocolates in a belly.
70 dogs in the garden barking.
70 cars at the front door parking.

70 birthdays in one year.
70 earrings in one ear.
70 calls on the ansaphone.
70 tigers with one bone.
70 sheep on the motorway.
70 taxis going away.
70 candles on one cake.
70 children with toothache.
70 monkeys in a car.
70 astronauts on a star.

70 wrinkles on a face.
70 miles in a race.
70 gherkins on a plate.
70 maggots for live bait.
70 crisp packets in the gutter.
70 ants in yellow butter.
70 Brussels sprouts for tea.
70 squirrels in a hazelnut tree.
70 moles on a putting-green.
70 heirs to the reigning Queen.

70 nuns in a taxi queue.
70 men in the ladies loo.
70 steps to the hangman's noose.
70 flies in the apple juice.
70 ferrets in a pair of jeans.
70 schoolboys eating beans.

70 kisses on the nose.
70 thorns on a blood-red rose.
70 sandwiches filled with cucumber.
70 ain't my favourite number.

3. I'VE GOT YOUR NUMBER

I've got your number.
It was on my pillow
when I woke up this morning.
It was yellow.

I held it in my hands.
It felt like a dry leaf.
I sniffed it cautiously.
It smelled of grief.

I've got your number.
It was in my bath
singing to itself in a rusty voice.
I heard its wheezy laugh.

I took it out and buried it
under the apple tree
but I looked back and saw it
following me.

Help me. Take it away.
I don't want it anymore.
I'm colder, older. It's getting dark.
I don't want to be 104.

4. What Mark did You Get?

I wrote a poem
that sang in the mouth
sweeter than wine.
79.

I painted a picture
that swam in the eye,
a serpentine.
79.

I played a tune
that rang in the ears
like something divine.
79.

I danced a dance
that sprang in the feet
like a chorus line.
79.

I lay in a box
that banged in the face
and was made of pine.
79.

_/_/99

Postman, postman, be as slow as you like
delivering this, your wobbling bike
barked down city streets, round country bends,
on your back a sack, bulging
with all our whispering, singing, yelling words
as the twentieth century ends.

In Nineteen Ninety-nine

It was a grey, airless Manchester day.
Your mother was sat in the back of a cab
on Princes Road, having just driven past
your brand new school and blown it a kiss.
You were four.

       Six motor bikes,
twirling their orange lights, whooping
their high alarms, roaring and revving, whizzed up
and cleared the whole of the carriageway
to your mother's right.

       She turned and looked
at the same time as the Queen,
in a huge and shining black limousine,
wearing a dress as red as your strawberry lollipop,
drew up – and for nearly a mile

       monarch and mum
queened it side by side in their separate cars.
Everyone flashed their lights! Everyone beeped their horns!
The day turned red and gold, magic and strange,
like a fairytale.

Counting to a Billion

In the year 2000,
he started by counting fleas.

In the year 2001,
he fingered the bees.

In 2002, he checked
the number of leaves on the trees.

By 2003, he was down on his knees
adding up grains of sand.

In 2004, he asked
for a show of hands.

In the year 2005,
he counted the rain,

drop by drop
and didn't stop

till 2006,
when he itemized snow,

flake by flake
without a break

till 2007,
which he spent counting baked beans,

. starting in Devon
and ending in Milton Keynes.

In the year 2008,
he totted up tears.

This took two years
and then, having made a mistake,

in 2010
he counted them all again.

In 2011,
he counted dogs;

in 2012,
he counted frogs.

In the year 2013,
he ticked off the birds in the sky.

In 2014,
he picked out the fish in the sea.

He counted balloons
in 2015

and in 2016
he counted spoons.

He counted mice
in 2017,

rats in 2018
and cats in 2019

and 2020,
which was plenty.

In the year 2021,
he counted eggs.

In the year 2022,
he reckoned up legs.

In 2023,
he took stock of stars

and in 2024
he counted some more

and again in 2025
and 2026.

By the end of 2027,
he'd finished with heaven.

In the year 2028,
he catalogued grapes.

In 2029
he tallied up bottles of wine —

and sipped from each one,
being thirsty.

In the year 2030,
he counted wasps.

In 2031,
he counted beetles.

In 2032,
he counted steeples.

In the year 2033, ,
he counted the dead,

but in 2034
there were more,

so, to count, in 2035,
you had to be alive.

In 2036,
he counted shops.

In 2037,
he counted ships.

In 2038,
he added up stones.

In 2039,
he tallied up phones.

In the year 2040,
he ran through mirrors.

In 2041,
he waded through rivers,

including brooks
and streams.

In 2042,
he counted books.

In 2043,
he counted dreams.

In 2044,
he numbered sheep.

In 2045,
he totalled hours spent asleep.

In 2046,
he added bricks.

In 2047,
he tallied sticks.

In 2048,
he counted children

and in 2049
he counted his millionth million.

By 2050 – BORED STIFF –
he'd reached a billion.

Zero

I tossed an imaginary coin,
nowt, nothing
up in the air
and watched it spinning there
like a copper leaf
blown by the puffed cheeks of the wind,
winning and losing,
heads or tails.
I caught it neat, pat
on the flat of my palm,
only the thought of a hole,
a notional O,
then went out to spend it.

What should I buy?
The plug on the sea bed,
pulled from the sand
by a mermaid's hand,
tossed to me as I stood on the shore
where I'd thrown my zero treasure
into the waves.
The ocean dwindled and gurgled away
like a bath
till only a puddle was left
where one fish swam.
Nothing can nothing buy
it sang.

So what could I buy?
The blue of the sky
swapped in a paint pot
for the not-a-lot I'd got.
The roof of the earth
was black and white
for a night and a day.
Then it was grey, grey, grey:
a washed-out shroud
to wrap up the world.
Out of it flew a bird on the wing.
Nowt owns nowt
I heard it sing.

Then what would I buy?
The velvet and satin purse of a Queen
dropped as she stepped
from her limousine
to the street.
Among the cheering and flashbulbs and flags
I stooped and popped
zilch
into her cloak.
But the Queen's swish purse
held only a rusty ring.
Nil gets nil
it started to sing.

So I went home
with a hole in the arse
of my pantaloons
and a head full of fairy tunes
to sit on the edge of my bed
and stare at the wall.
Round, like zero, shone
the light of the face of the sun.
Round, like zero, shone
the light of the face of the moon.
In my empty palm, round, like zero,
brightest of all there shone
nothing at all.

The Moon

One day, a new girl came to our school
and she was The Moon. Shy at first,
she sat at the back of the class.
I saw how silver edged her blazer,
moonlight round a cloud.

                     At break,
eating an apple, The Moon sat alone
on a bench. I went up to say hello.
Her amber eyes stared into mine. A halo
seemed to hoop-la her hair. *Do you dare,*
she said, *to make friends with The Moon?*

I did. All that year, I went everywhere
with The Moon. Swimming she liked, floating
around and gazing up at the sky.
And Poetry; she'd laugh with delight
at the similes for herself. She loved
to eat – cheese, bananas, melons – and feared
balloons, in case they burst in her face.

The Moon was top of the class
in Geography, History, Languages, Art,
in Music, Science, Maths; said
there was really nothing new under the sun
and grinned. She was modest, though,
so nobody seemed to mind.
I was proud to be The Moon's best friend.

She disappeared on the School Trip
to the beach. I saw her skimming stones
at the edge of the sea, then wandered off by myself
to look for shells. They searched till night fell,
till a full moon dragged the tide
over her name in the sand.

                Next term,
a new pupil sat at The Moon's desk.
Nobody said a word. The clocks went back
and walking home from school in the dark
I sometimes saw the moon in the sky,
now like a secret smile, now like a friendly laugh,
now like an amber eye.

The Good Friend
of Melanie Moon

For the first year of my friendship with Melanie Moon
I gave her a cotton worm.
In the second year I gave her a paper spoon.
For the third, a leather piano.
For the fourth, a rose.
In the fifth year of my friendship with Melanie Moon
I gave her a wooden glove.
Year six, an iron hanky.
Year seven, a woollen book.
Year eight, a bronze banana.
Year nine, a copper hat.
In the tenth year of my friendship with Melanie Moon
I gave her a tin cat.

In year eleven I gave her slippers of steel.
In year twelve I gave her a silk cheroot.
A lace knife in thirteen.
In fourteen, an ivory wasp.
In the fifteenth year of my friendship with Melanie Moon
I gave her a crystal moth.

Melanie Moon – in our twentieth year I gave her a china car.

Melanie Moon – in our twenty-fifth year
I gave her
a silver tent.
In the thirtieth year, a pearl pear.
In year thirty-five, a coral cake.
In the fortieth year, a ruby boot.
In year forty-five, a sapphire goat.

Melanie, Melanie, Melanie Moon,
in our fiftieth year a golden umbrella.
Melanie, Melanie, Melanie Moon,
in our fifty-fifth year an emerald gun.
In the sixtieth year of our friendship
I gave her a diamond balloon
and then my friendship with Melanie Moon
was over and done.

Friends

Miss Thunder, Miss Lightning, met in the sky:
Delighted to meet you!
Likewise, I!
Do you take hail in your tea?
I do.
One lump or two?

Miss River, Miss Meadow, met on the ground:
Lovely to see you!
Greetings, well found!
Do you like mud on your crumpet?
I'll try it
stuff the diet.

Miss Ocean, Miss Hurricane, met out at sea:
Look who's blown in!
It's only me.
Do you like foam on your coffee?
Why not!
And chocolate?

Miss Cloud, Miss Moon, met in the dark:
Let's make a night of it!
Just say the word!
How do you like your puddle?
Shaken,
not stirred.

Miss Fog, Miss Road, met on a walk:
Long time no see!
I've been abroad.
Will you have salt on your soup?
I'd better.
Pass the pepper.

Miss Frost, Miss Grass, met in a garden:
Hello Stranger!
I do beg your pardon!
Do you like ice in your drink?
I love it —
and lemon!

Miss Wind, Miss Tumbleweed, met out East
Yoo-hoo! Yoo-hoo!
You can't catch me!
Let me pour you some tea.
Do you take it with sand?
Four heaped spoonfuls would be grand!

Miss Darkness, Miss Silence, met at night:
Fancy some cocoa?
That would be nice.
One marshmallow each?
Then we'll put out
the light.

Brave Enough

I wonder would you be my closest friend
if I was brave enough
to tie the ribbons of your dress to mine
and run like girl and shadow, shade and girl,
across the grass.

                I wonder
would you climb into this tree
if I was brave enough to toss an apple down
from where I watch you on your way to school
and sit beside me on the branch

                        swinging your legs
as, brave enough, I'd say *Let's stay*
forever in this tree, girl and shadow, shade and girl,
you and me, and not grow older, richer, wiser, sadder
by one day. I wonder what you'd say.

Girl and Tree

A girl fell in love with a tree
and a tree with a girl.
Holding the tree in her arms, the girl said
Tree, I love you best in the world.
Why, said the tree, *do you love me so?*
Because of the green of your leaves, said the girl.

The girl climbed up into the tree
and sat on a branch, dangling her legs.
Girl, girl, I love you best, believe me please,
whispered the tree.
Why, said the girl, *do you love best me?*
Because of your cherry-red dress, said the tree.

Then the wind blew and the tree's green sails
breathed and gasped and filled with air
and the wood of the tree creaked like a ship
and the girl was Captain there.

Only the moon, agog with light,
saw the girl and the tree that night
when the whole town, in full pursuit,
came with dogs and searched the woods
where a smiling girl in a cherry-red dress
slept in the arms of a tree, like fruit.

A Crow and a Scarecrow

A crow and a scarecrow fell in love
out in the fields.
The scarecrow's heart was a stuffed leather glove
but his love was real.
The crow perched on the stick of a wrist
and opened her beak:
Scarecrow, I love you madly, deeply.
Speak.

Crow, rasped the Scarecrow, *hear these words*
from my straw throat.
I love you too
from my boot to my hat
by way of my old tweed coat.
Croak.
The crow crowed back,
Scarecrow, let me take you away
to live in a tall tree.
I'll be a true crow wife to you
if you'll marry me.

The Scarecrow considered.
Crow, tell me how
a groom with a broomstick spine
can take a bride.
I know you believe in the love
in these button eyes
but I'm straw inside
and straw can't fly.

The crow pecked at his heart
with her beak
then flapped away,
and back and forth she flew to him
all day, all day,
until she pulled one last straw
from his tattered vest
and soared across the sun with it
to her new nest.

And there she slept, high in her tree,
winged, in a bed of love.
Night fell.
The slow moon rose
over a meadow,
a heap of clothes,
two boots,
an empty glove.

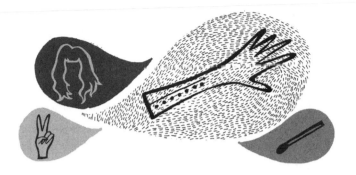

The Glove

I started off silk, the colour of milk, with a pearly sheen,
and graced the waving hand of a much-loved Queen
till her lady-in-waiting noticed a stain and passed me on
to a palace maid who wore me, once, on her wedding-day

then threw me away as she tossed her bouquet

into the smiling crowd. I was caught, washed, pressed
and starched by a pickpocketing girl, who sheathed
her hand in my fingers and thumb and dipped
into jackets, pockets, purses, bags, till fairly copped

by the boys in blue. You-Know-Who was Exhibit One,

next to a replica gun and a long blonde wig. After
the guilty plea, a show of repentance, suspended
sentence, she walked clear, but Muggins here was swiped
by a cop, scrunched in his mitt, and used to wipe

the mist from his windscreen, ending up in the boot

with a crumpled three-piece suit and a ketchuped shirt. Taken
to the cleaners, chucked in a box marked *Lost and Found*,
I was bought for a pound by a lad who needed a show
of hand to stick on the empty wrist of the arm of his Guy –

it was Bonfire Night. The Queen lit a fuse. Yours Truly

fingered a Churchill Victory 'V' as the fireworks boasted
and swaggered about in the overhead dark. It was then
that I overheard a remark from the Queen's true heir: *Ma'am
and Mama! Regard the glove on the Guy on the top*

of the pyre! It's pair to the one at home that lies on its own

on a cushion next to the throne! Then the Prince himself
ordered the match, that was lit and ready to lick my digits clean
to the bone, blown out, and I was carried home by him,
to be soaped by servants, shampooed, perfumed, back

to the glove I'd been on the hand of a waving, reigning Queen.

Gifts

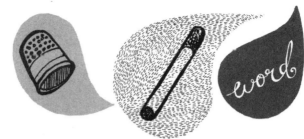

1. A CIGARETTE

A friend of mine gave me a cigarette.

I put it unlit in a saucer and went to my bed.
When I got up it had grown to the size of a wand.
A magic wand to turn folk into smoke.
A friend of mine gave me a cigarette.

I popped it into a jamjar and sloped to the swings.
When I came back it had grown to the size of a stick.
A white stick to use when you cannot see.
A friend of mine gave me a cigarette.

I stuck it into the ground and went to my room.
When I looked out it had grown to the size of a tree.
A tree weeping its leaves over a grave.
A friend of mine gave me a cigarette.

I climbed to the top for most of the following day.
When I looked down it had grown to the size of a beanstalk.
A beanstalk finding a coughing giant in the clouds.
A friend of mine gave me a cigarette.

I tried to jump off but by now the thing was on fire.
When I looked round it had grown to the size of a death.
A death that definitely wasn't going to be mine. You bet . . .
No friend of mine gave me a cigarette.

2. The Word

A friend gave me the Word,
said *Pass it on.*
But I kept the word to myself for seven days.
At the end of a week it had grown to the length of a phrase.

A friend gave me a phrase,
said *Spread it about.*
But I kept the phrase at home to watch it lengthen.
By the end of the week it had stretched to the size of a sentence.

A friend gave me a sentence,
said *Shout it loud.*
But by now I was keeping it in. It lived in the bath.
By the end of the following week it had swelled to a paragraph.

A friend gave me a paragraph,
said *Set it to music.*
But it had the keys to the house, it had come of age.
At the end of the week it had spread to the width of a page.

A friend gave me a page,
said *Paint it large.*
But the page was bulging, daily fatter and fatter.
By the end of that week it had beefed itself up to a chapter.

A friend gave me the word,
said *Tell all the World.*
But the word was alive and the word had grown to a book.
This is it. Look.

3. A Silver Thimble

A boy in Needlework
gave me a silver thimble.
It grew overnight to the size of a quaich.
What could I use it for now?
For drinking milkshake!

A boy in Latin
gave me a stick of chalk.
It grew overnight to a road.
What could I use it for now?
To go for a walk!

A boy in Maths
gave me some blotting paper.
It grew overnight to the size of an acre.
What could I use it for now?
To grow potatoes!

A boy in Geography
gave me a globe.
It grew overnight to the size of Mars.
What could I use it for now?
To visit the stars!

A boy in P.E.
gave me a kiss.
It grew overnight to the size of Undying Love.
What can I use it for now?
(Can anyone actually give me any advice about this?)

Ask Oscar

Dear Oscar,
I stay up too late
the night before an exam
trying to cram.
What do you advise?

Revise.

Dear Oscar,
I have fallen in love
with a girl in my class at school.
I feel such a fool!
What should I do?

Woo.

Dear Oscar,
I am prone to spots   lots!
What can you suggest please?

Squeeze.

Dear Oscar,
I keep seeing a ghost
on the stairs.
Are ghosts real
or am I being foolish?

Ghoulish.

Dear Oscar,
there are so many faiths
in the world.
Which, in your view,
is The One?

None.

Dear Oscar,
I want to be a poet!
Please tell me how
if you can spare the time.

Rhyme.

A Rhyme

I went out on my own for a roam
and bumped into a rhyme.
Come back to my room,
it begged, it cajoled. *I'm lonely.*
I'll pour you a tot of rum
and pour out my story.

Its room was covered in grime,
it was grim;
but I settled down with my dram
as though in a dream.
It's a crying shame!
sobbed the rhyme –

It's a crime
that a rhyme in its prime,
who has often heard
midnight's bells chime,
should be left without even a crumb
or a spoonful of cream.

Then it started to name
the poems it knew in its time,
like a manager picking his team,
like the boastful beat of a drum,
like the count of a difficult sum,
and its eyes filled up to the brim.

I tried to say something, to seem
as if life wasn't all doom and gloom.
But the rhyme wasn't dumb,
knew my game,
and sobbed even more all the same:
I had money and power and fame –

Now I'm out on a limb
with no buddy to spare me a dime.
Suddenly, out of the window,
weeping, it started to climb –
then I heard it hit the ground
with a sickening rhyme.

Translation

Here's an interesting rhyme:
once upon a time,
a translator mistook *vair*
(which means sable) for *verre*
(which means glass).
Silly fella!
      And so Cinderella,
her slipper a furry tail,
was trapped in a fairytale
(no translator being dafter)
happily
        ever
           after.

Dimples

When I'm scared the Monsters are thrilling me.
When I'm cold the North Wind is chilling me.
When I'm pretty some ribbons are frilling me.
When I'm fibbing my teacher is grilling me.
When I'm sad my salt tears are spilling free.
When I'm brave my courage is willing me.
When I fidget my Grandma is stilling me.
When I'm hungry my Mother is filling me.
When I'm spending the toy shop is billing me.
When I score the referee's nilling me.
When I'm ill the doctor is pilling me.
When it's dawn the sparrows are trilling me.
But when I laugh and laugh and laugh and laugh
and laugh MY DIMPLES ARE KILLING ME!

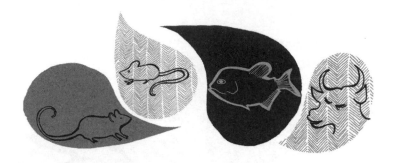

Irish Rats Rhymed to Death

It was once a common belief that rats in pasturages could be destroyed by anathematizing them in rhyming verse or by metrical charms . . .

Do you want to get rid of an Irish rat?
I can advise how to go about that.
Take a deep breath
and rhyme it to death:
Look, rat!
There goes a cat in a new hat!
Get lost, rat!
There isn't a WELCOME for you on this mat.
Rot to a skeleton, ratty old rat.
You're fat.

Do you want to get shut of a Scottish mouse?
I can advise how to de-mouse your house.
Take a deep breath
and rhyme it to death:
See, mouse!
A louse is itching away in a grouse.
Go away, mouse!
We don't want you here a-nibbling our house.
Watch out for the cheese in the trap, mousy mouse.
Use your nous.

Do you want to be shot of an English fish?
I can advise how to fulfil your wish.
Take a deep breath
and rhyme it to death:
Oy, fish!
There's a pool of pish in this dish.
Scram, fish!
You're wet. Your mouth is an O,
your tail is a swish.
We've got a good idea, fishy fish,
we'll eat you with chips.

Do you want to be free of a Welsh cow?
I can advise exactly how.
Take a deep breath
and rhyme it to death:
How now, cow!
A dancing sow is taking a bow.
Disappear, cow!
Your udders are bagpipes making a row.
Put a plug in that *Moo*, cowy cow.
Do it now.

Let's all have one last rhyme for the cow:
Pow-wow!
(And one for the rat-
SPLAT!)

Opposites

The opposite of worry is umbrella.
The opposite of camel is paella.
The opposite of sneeze
and the opposite of trees
is, respectively, rumbaba and goodfella.

The opposite of children is confetti.
The opposite of monkey is spaghetti.
The opposite of goat
and the opposite of boat,
as most folks know, is wellington and yeti.

The opposite of caravan is green.
The opposite of jellyfish is queen.
The opposite of fridge
and the opposite of midge
is antidisestablishmentarianism and bean.

The opposite of toe is kangaroo.
The opposite of nostril is kazoo.
The opposite of wood
and the opposite of good
is, no bout adoubt it, zoo and stew.

The opposite of someone else is me.
The opposite of skeleton is thee.
The opposite of crazy
and the opposite of lazy
is definitely us and maybe we.

The Sock

Most feet stink
and those that don't,
unfortunately,
pong.

Dang ding.
Dang ding.
Dang ding.
Dang ding dong.

You wouldn't think
there's much
to being a sock.
You would be wrong.

Dang ding.
Dang ding.
Dang ding.
Dang ding dong.

What's dang?
What's ding?
You're asking.
It's my song.

Dang ding.
Dang ding.
Dang ding.
Dang ding dong.

Crikey Dick

to Camilla and Beatrice

I've eaten too much chocolate, I feel sick.
The stink of snuffed-out candles gets my wick.
There's a scab upon my knee I want to pick.
I cannot do my homework, I'm too thick.
There's only one thing for it – CRIKEY DICK!

I've stuffed myself with pizza, now I'm ill.
My mark out of a hundred's always nil.
The medicine I take's a bitter pill.
I feel so stressed although I want to chill.
There's only one thing for it – BLIMEY PHIL!

There's never any ink inside my pen.
There's never any Nevis on my Ben.
There's never any egg inside my hen.
I stop at seven when I count to ten.
There's only one thing for it – LUMME LEN!

There's only one thing for it – LUMME LEN!
There's only one thing for it – BLIMEY PHIL!
So when you feel like shouting BLOODY HELL!
or smashing through a window with a brick –
there's only one thing for it – CRIKEY DICK!

Not Not Nursery Rhymes

1 COOL, KIND BUNS

Cool, kind buns.
Cool, kind buns.
Very many?
Hardly any
Cool, kind buns.

2 THREE SHARP-SIGHTED MICE

Three sharp-sighted mice,
Three sharp-sighted mice.
See how they run!
See how they run!
They're all avoiding the farmer's wife –
She's slit his throat with a carving knife.
They've never seen so much blood in their life –
Those three sharp-sighted mice.

3 HUMPTY DUMPTY

Humpty Dumpty stood on one leg.
Humpty Dumpty was only an egg.
All the King's horses
And all the King's men
Had to have omelette for dinner again.

4 JACK AND JILL

Jill and Jill went up the hill
To fetch themselves a daughter.
Jack and Jack were coming back,
And all of them did what they oughta.

5 HO DOODLE DOODLE

Ho doodle doodle,
The rat and the poodle
Were quarrelling over a bone.
An elephant came
and told me their game
in a text from its mobile phone.

Inside the Egg

Inside the egg, unheard,
was a bird.

Inside the bird, unsung,
was a song.

Inside the song, mute,
was a flute.

Inside the flute, wound,
was the wind.

Inside the wind, freed,
was a seed.

Inside the seed, wee,
was a tree.

Inside the tree, trapped,
was sap.

Inside the sap, tight,
was light.

Inside the light, bright,
was sight.

Inside the sight, clear,
was a tear.

Inside the tear, salty,
was sea.

Inside the sea, afloat,
was a boat.

Inside the boat, locked,
was a box.

Inside the box, wrapped,
was a map.

Inside the map, true,
was a clue.

Inside the clue, concealed,
was a field.

Inside the field, hush,
was a bush.

Inside the bush, alive,
was a hive.

Inside the hive, unseen,
was a queen.

Inside the queen, runny,
was honey.

Inside the honey, soon,
was a spoon.

Inside the spoon, old,
was gold.

Inside the gold, slim,
was a ring.

Inside the ring, pinker,
was a finger.

Inside the finger, thin,
was a pin.

Inside the pin, worse,
was a curse.

Inside the curse, twitch,
was a witch.

Inside the witch, queer,
was a fear.

Inside the fear, bragging,
was a dragon.

Inside the dragon, dire,
was a fire.

Inside the fire, remembered,
were embers.

Inside the embers, charred,
was a word.

Inside the word, look,
was a book.

Inside the book, at home,
was a poem.

Inside the poem, curled,
was a world.

Inside the world, of course,
was a horse.

Inside the horse, whole,
was a foal.

Inside the foal, wallop,
was a gallop.

Inside the gallop, wild,
was a mile.

Inside the mile, good,
was a wood.

Inside the wood, at rest,
was a nest.

Inside the nest, peek,
was a beak.

Inside the beak, sung,
was a song.

Inside the song, heard,
was a bird.

Inside the bird, big,
was an egg.

F For Fox

The fox fled over the fields away from the farm
and the furious farmer.
His fur was freaked.
His foxy face was frantic as he flew. A few feathers
fluttered out of his mouth.
The fox
had broken his fast with a feast of fowl!
The farmer had threatened to flay the fur
from his frame.
The frightened fox flung himself
at a fence.

The fox found himself in a fairground,
with a Ferris Wheel, flashing lights, fruit machines, fish
in plastic bags.
Furtively, he foraged for food –
fragments of candy floss, French fries –
but a fella folding fivers into his fist
flicked a fiery fag at the fox and the fox foxed off.

Further and further fled the fox, through Forfar, Fife, Falkirk,
forests, fields, Fleetwood, Fazakerley, thunder and fog,
famished and fearful;
forcing his furry features
into family bins, filching thrown-away food.
Thief fox, friendless fox, thin fox. Finally
he came at first light to a faraway farm . . .

where the fox fed himself full
till his face was fat
and forlorn feathers floated away on the frosty air.

Nippy Maclachlan

Nippy Maclachlan lives at the Border, the place
where language changes with water,
where flooers grow thistles and thustles grow flowers,
and eagles fly high clutching takeaway mice.
Nippy Maclachlan is nasty, not nice.

Nippy Maclachlan lives on the wire, the fence
between air, earth, water and fire, where milk in a coo
soors in the udder, if one acre's one man's, the other's
his brother's, where foxes' sly jaws are feathery, bloody.
Nippy Maclachlan's smelly and muddy.

Nippy Maclachlan lives at the crossing, the point
where everything has to reverse,
where rain turns to thunder and thunder to worse
and rats crawl on their bellies through sewer and ditch.
Nippy Maclachlan has warts and a twitch.

Nippy Maclachlan sharpens her stones, flings them
at folk who are far from their homes,
spits and hangs ribbons of phlegm on the wind,
snogs with a scarecrow out in the fields.
Do you think Nippy Maclachlan is real?

Ran Out of Sugar

Ran out of sugar – went next door,
asked the cat for a cup. Can't,
she purred, run out of cream.
Teamed up – went next door, asked
the dog for a jug. No way, he barked,
run out of tea. So we poor three
went next door, asked the cow
for a caddy. Can't, she mooed,
run out of toast. Four strong,
we went next door, asked the fox
for a loaf. Can't, he drawled, run out
of butter. Five now, went next door,
asked the sheep for a pat. Can't, she baaed,
run out of jam. Formed a gang and went next door,
asked the pig for a jar. Can't, he squealed,
run out of honey. Wasn't funny. Went next door,
asked the horse for a comb. Nay, he neighed,
run out of eggs. Thirty legs went next door,

asked the goat for a carton. Can't, he cursed,
run out of bacon. Nine now, went next door
and asked the rat for a rasher. Can't, he spat,
run out of sausage. Ten proud, went next door,
asked the hare for a link. Can't, he lisped,
run out of mustard. First XI went next door,
asked the hen for a scrape. Can't, she clucked,
run out of pepper. Dozen of us went next door,
asked the mouse for a mill. Can't, she squeaked,
run out of soup. Formed a line, went next door,
asked the mule for a bowl. Can't, he brayed,
run out of cake. Went next door, asked the bull
for a slice. Can't, he snorted, run out of ale.
Fifty-six legs trailed next door, asked the frog
for a pint. Can't, he croaked, run out of nuts.
Fifteen tuts. Went next door. We were back
at mine. Still no sugar. Ran out of wine.

Toy Dog

for Matthew Kay

When I come home from school, he doesn't bark.
He doesn't fetch the stick I throw for him in Clissold Park,
or bite a burglar's ankle in the dark.
Toy dog.

When I wake up he doesn't lick my face.
He never beats me by a mile the times we have a race,
or digs a bone up from his secret place.
Toy dog.

When I say *Heel!* or *Sit!* he can't obey.
I buy a red dog-collar for him, though he will not stray,
or trip me up at soccer when I play.
Toy dog.

One day his brown glass eyes will soften, see.
One night, his nylon tail will wag when I come in for tea;
his cloth leg cock against a lamp-post for a pee.
Good dog.

Begged

He begged for a dog
with four fur paws,
with a bark and a wag
and a wet nose,
with a collar and lead and a drinking-bowl,
with a full-moon howl;
he begged, begged,
begged for a hound
with a cocked-leg and a grin and a growl,
with a basket, a blanket, a bone,
with a feeding-dish
and tricks with a ball,
a dog that would fetch and sit and heel.

He got his wish,
awoke in the black and barking dark –
the moon like a fang
in the mouth of night –
and, terrified, turned on the light:
smile of a wolf,
yeti's paws at his neck,
yard of tongue, pink, wet,
butcher's breath.
He felt like death,
he felt sick,
then he felt the first fierce frantic lick
of the dog's dog love.

A love that sobbed
if he left the room,
clawed and scratched
at the closing door,
puked on the floor,
howled and yowled fit to wake the dead
till it shared his bed –
man's best friend's head
on the pillow,
eyes rolled back in their sockets,
blind, yellow.
Good dog, good chap, good boy,
good fellow . . .

He longed for a good night's sleep,
a bath, a quiet meal
or a TV dinner,
an hour with a book.
He grew haggard, thinner,
but at his heel
the hound grew huge,
padded along
with the *News* in its jaws,
sat at his feet like a welcome mat
till he begged –
how he begged –
for a gerbil, a tortoise, a hamster, a rabbit, a goldfish, a cat.

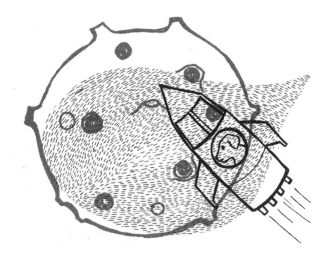

There's a Dog

There's a dog in a spaceship orbiting Mars.
There's a dog with its paw on the wheel of a car.
There's a dog born under a lucky star.
There's a dog.

There's a dog fast asleep in the bed of the Queen.
There's a dog autographing its name with a pen.
There's a dog in the sea in a submarine.
There's a dog.

There's a dog that doesn't eat socks and shoes.
There's a dog that hasn't got nothing to lose.
There's a dog that doesn't how-ow-owl the blues.
There's a dog.

There's a dog reading poetry under a lamp.
There's a dog's dog face on a first class stamp.
There's a dog out jogging despite its limp.
There's a dog.

There's a dog in the kitchen cooking a meal.
There's a dog with wings at God's right heel.
There's a dog hang-gliding in a Force 10 gale.
There's a dog.

There's a dog that doesn't chew table legs.
There's a dog that never whines and begs.
There's a dog that hasn't grown too big.
There's a dog.

There's a dog in goal at the FA Cup.
There's a dog teaching French to a newborn pup.
There's a dog in the City on the up-and-up.
There's a dog.

There's a dog in the charts at Number One.
There's a dog in charge at Number Ten.
There's a dog playing chance on number nine.
There's a dog.

There's a dog that doesn't bite small boys.
There's a dog that doesn't swallow toys.
There's a dog that doesn't bark at the slightest noise.
There's a dog.

There's a dog. There's a dog.
There's a dog. There's a dog.
There's a dog that DOESN'T LIVE WITH US.

Glad

Glad we don't have to bark.
Glad we don't have to cock
one leg and wee on a lamppost.
Glad we don't have to cluck
or lay an egg. Glad we don't
have to moo, neigh, baa, eat grass
or hay, be milked, fleeced, ridden.
Glad we don't have to hoot, hang
from the thread of a web, sting, slither.
Glad we don't have to mew, eat mice,
peck, breathe through gills, dwell
in shells or form a chrysalis, hiss,
hum, hover. Glad we don't
have to kip upside down in the dark, bark.

So Shy

He was so shy he was born with a caul,
sort of a shawl made from the membrane
of the womb. He was tongue-tied;

so shy he kept a dummy in his mouth
for two years; then, when that went,
a thumb. He was wide-eyed, dumb; so shy

he would hide in the cupboard under the stairs
for hours, with a bear; hearing his name called
from the top to the bottom of the house, quiet

as a sugar-mouse; shy as the milk in a coconut,
shy as a slither of soap. When he got dressed,
he wore shy clothes – a balaclava, mitts.

He ate shy food – blancmange, long-lasting mints.
He drank shy drinks – juice from a cup
with a lid and a lip, sip by shy sip.

He was so shy he lived with a blush,
sort of a flush under the skin, like the light
behind curtains on windows when somebody's in.

The piano eats with chop sticks,
cool minims,
diced demi-semiquavers.

When the lid goes down,
the piano is inscrutable,
shining with health.

The piano stands politely
until the next meal, silent
for as long as it takes.

Chocs

Into the half-pound box of Moonlight
my small hand crept.
There was an electrifying rustle.
There was a dark and glamorous scent.
Into my open, religious mouth
the first Marzipan Moment went.

Down in the crinkly second layer
five finger-piglets snuffled
among the Hazelnut Whirl,
the Caramel Swirl,
the Black Cherry and Almond Truffle.

Bliss.

I chomped, I gorged.
I stuffed my face,
till only the Coffee Cream
was left for the owner of the box –
tough luck, Ann Pope –
oh, and half an Orange Supreme.

Fishcakes

Every Friday night, through rain or snow
through fog or thunder and lightning
a man in a cloak
with a royal flag
on a coal-black horse came riding.
He stopped at a shop
in Stafford Town
where the window glittered with fish
stood in his stirrups,
flung down a purse
and red-faced bellowed this:

Fishcakes! Fishcakes! Fishcakes for the Queen!
Fishcakes for the Queen of England!

Now some know hope,
some know despair,
and some what difference a wish makes –
but the nightly dream
of the rightful Queen
was of six grilled Stafford fishcakes.

Away he sped, cowl on head,
fishcakes under his arm,
past town and village, field and stream,
past croft, cottage, farm.
The cream of a stone of top-class spuds,
a salmon prince and his bride
mixed with breadcrumbs, parsley, chives
were soon to be inside
the Queen. *Fishcakes! Fishcakes!*
Fishcakes for the Queen!
Fishcakes for the Queen of England!

Some know the grind
of a dog with a bone,
some know the smash when a dish breaks –
but nowt compared
to the noise on the throne
of the Queen gobbling up her fishcakes.

Grandma Barr's Cherry Tomatoes

Grandma Barr loved cherry tomatoes.
Ten red tomatoes in a sky-blue bowl
shone on the window ledge in Grandma's kitchen.
I'll have two now in a warm bread roll,
thought Grandma Barr, buttering away.
But when she looked, there were only eight
of her favourite tomatoes
glowing on the ledge in their own cool bowl.

Out in the yard was a pot of basil.
I'll pick some of that
then I'll chop up a shallot,
thought Grandma Barr,
and with five of the tomatoes
I'll make myself a salad and a pot of tea.
But when she checked, there were less of the tomatoes
left than she'd reckoned – only one, two, three.

Grandma Barr slept in a nightdress
embroidered with tomatoes on the cuffs and hem.
There were only three tomatoes
in the darkness of her kitchen,
so all night long she dreamt of them:
the furry seeds
ticking in their centres,
the feel and the taste and the scent of them.

Breakfast time —
the sun was an egg
cracked from its shell
in the saucer of the sky.
Grandma Barr was hungry.
She fancied three tomatoes
salted and peppered on a toasted slice of rye.
But where there'd been three
there were no tomatoes
to be found in the bowl on the window ledge,
not a sniff, not a hint, not the ghost of a tomato.
This is very very strange,
Grandma Barr said,
with a puzzled, worried shake
of her old white head.

Was a Lad

We didn't eat sweets when I was a lad,
we ate dust.
We walked on our feets when I was a lad,
there was no bus.
There was no fuss when I was a lad,
no fuss.

We didn't wear clothes when I was a lad,
we wore rags.
We had no shoes when I was a lad,
we had clogs.
There were no hugs when I was a lad,
no hugs.

We didn't play games when I was a lad,
we played dead.
We had no names when I was a lad,
there was no need.
There was no bread when I was a lad,
no bread.

We didn't drink Coke when I was a lad,
we drank rain.
We never felt sick when I was a lad,
there was no pain.
There was no phone when I was a lad,
no phone.

We didn't we never when I was a lad,
we had no say.
We hadn't we couldn't when I was a lad,
there was no pay.
There wasn't we shouldn't when I was a lad,
no way.

The Red Skeleton

Down in the graveyard where everyone's dead
dwells a skeleton whose bones are red.
She's different from the other ghouls.
Their bones are whiter than an oyster's pearls,
than a baby's tooth,
than nothing but the truth,
than a ghost's two legs,
but the oddball skeleton's bones are red.

Down in the damp of a tombstone bed
kips a skeleton whose tibia is red,
her fibula too (no word of a lie).
Most bones are as white,
when their owners die,
as vanilla ice cream on apple pie,
as the first grey hair on a middle-aged head,
but the lone shark skeleton's bones are red.

When she lived she loved tomatoes,
shiny apples, peppers, sweet potatoes,
watermelons, raspberries, damson jam,
eggs paprika in the frying pan, plums, pomegranates,
ketchup, wine. She loved each moment
of her flesh-and-blood time
from crimson sunset to strawberry cone
and she shows that love with her dead red bones.

Cuddling Skeletons

Cuddling skeletons huddled up dead
skull to skull in a dark dirt bed.
A worm crawled in through the first one's nose,
reappeared near the second ones's toes.
Hold me tight with your cold white bones.

Huddling skeletons cuddled up dead.
Neither could hear what the other one said.
Ears were peepholes, tongues were mush –
so who sang the lullaby *Wheesht . . . Hush . . .*
I'll hold you tight with my cold white bones?

Cuddling skeletons muddled-up bits,
coccyges, femurs, elbows, hips,
tibias, fibulas, kneecaps, spines –
That rib's your one, this rib's mine.
Hold me tight with your cold white bones.

Muddling skeletons cuddled up, pleased
at the bony scrape of the other one's knees.
They grinned in the mud, clasping hands,
pale long fingers like magic wands.
I'll hold you tight with my cold white bones.

Cuddling skeletons huddled up dead,
a spinning spider in each cave head.
A young girl came with yellow flowers
for the stone up above in the living hours.
Hold me tight with your cold white bones.

I'll hold you tight with my cold white bones.

Skeleton, Moon, Poet

Three Found Poems from the Web

1 SKELETON

A skeleton is not a secret.
A skeleton might growl.
A skeleton does not dance on tables.
A skeleton does like to be petted.
A skeleton is ferocious.
A skeleton is considered man's best friend.
A skeleton stinks.
A skeleton is hazardous to your health.
A skeleton is found in a bathroom.
A skeleton is fluffy.
A skeleton probably doesn't chirp.

2 Moon

The moon is not awake at night.
The moon does not jump.
The moon does not come in many varieties.
The moon does not burn your tongue when eaten.
The moon does not swim.
The moon cannot be hunted.
The moon is not dangerous.
The moon does not help one accomplish tasks.
The moon is not capricious.
You cannot hold the moon.
The moon is not worth a lot of money.
You would be lost without the moon.

3 Poet

A poet might not be chewed.
People might not sit on a poet.
You cannot peel a poet.
A poet is probably not combustible.
You might not use a poet to hit something.
A poet is probably not animal feed.
A poet is probably not used in Oriental cooking.
A poet is probably not crunchy.
A poet might not be used to talk to others.
A poet probably doesn't coo.
A poet doesn't provide protection.

Going On the Web

The Web was slung
from the lowest branch of the wishing-tree
to the garden fence,
was different from the average web,
was immense, glittering in the lemony evening April light.
Now – I had never been on the Web
in my life
but I climbed on, surprising myself,
and wobbled along the tightrope walk
of the lowest silver strand
then managed to grab the rope above
and pull myself up.

I was on the Web!
I leaned on a bridge
and a thousand glimmering motorways
shimmered below,
speeding, winking away
as far as the eye could see.
Some roads aimed high,
seemed to take off and fly,
to pitch themselves
at a distant star
and arrive like surf
on a faraway beach.

I dived from my high wire
into the sea,
that great briny restless churn of a mind
with its singing whales,
mime-artist fish, writerly oysters
polishing up their poems of pearls;
the genius sea
flat on its back to stare at the moon,
the trampoline moon.
I bounced and I flew,
watching the lost blue ball of the earth
rolling through space.
I named each place –

Africa – where tigers burned
and turned to butter under a storybook sun.
India – elephants moving along like clouds of stone.
Mount Everest – climbers were broken dolls
left out on the slopes.
The North Pole,
China's wall,
Niagara Falls,
The Taj Mahal.
My English home – a flickering web
in a garden there, flagged from a tree.

I fell to the grass
with a bump,
a moth dusting my cheek,
and I saw stars
like fistfuls of rice
thrown to the universe,
the Web expanding and stretching out
till it disappeared
into all the dark and breathing air of the world
leaving only a girl,
her mother whistling her in from the chill of the moon.

Safe Sounds

You like safe sounds:
the dogs lapping at their bowls;
the pop of a cork on a bottle of plonk
as your mother cooks;
the *Match of the Day* theme tune
and *Doctor Who-oo-oo*.

                Safe sounds:
your name called, two happy syllables
from the bottom to the top of the house;
your daft ring tone; the low gargle
of hot water in bubbles. Half asleep
in the drifting boat of your bed,
you like to hear the big trees
sound like the sea instead.

Sweet Homes

If I was warm and safe
I wouldn't tut
or turn my nose up
at a little hut.

*

With Marian
and Robin's Merrie Men
I'd be convivial and cheerful
in a den.

*

A garden sack
as pillow for my head,
I'd get a good night's kip
inside a shed.

*

With flap for much-loved cat
(therefore no mouse)
I'd settle quietly down
in my own house.

*

One's coat of arms
displayed upon a banner,
I'd lord it as the lady
of the Manor.

*

But best of all
I wouldn't have no hassle
were I installed and walled up
in a castle.

Secrets

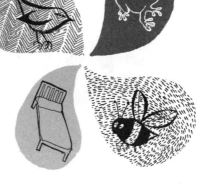

High on the branch of a tree,
a bird in its nest chirped:
I grasp what I grasp.
A secret's a worm that hides
in the earth, slides about in the gloom,
sifting the whispering soil
where flowers unwrap.

Down by the bright green pond,
a frog on its lily croaked:
I ken what I ken.
A secret's a dragonfly key
locking, unlocking, the air
where silvery fish jump high
for the hooks of the fishermen.

Out in the shimmering meadow,
a bee in a flower buzzed:
I suss what I suss.
Blown on a breeze,
a secret's a dusting of pollen
carried downwind in the sunlight
to end in a sneeze.

Snug in her bed in her room,
a child in her blankets crooned:
I know what I know.
A secret's a shadow thrown on a wall,
all fingers and thumbs,
which dances, dances for me
till the darkness comes.

Star and Moon

for Helen Taylor

An unborn child slept
in the gleam of a star.
A childless mother tossed and turned
on a moon.
High over the moon
the chuckling light of the star.
Beneath the star
the milky glow of the moon.

An unborn child
fell through the dark
like a shooting star.
A mother held out her arms
on the highest hill of the moon.
There you are!
Yes, I am coming soon!
Little Star singing to Mama Moon.

Then a child was born
and she slept
on the breast of the moon.
And a mother's arms were filled
with the light of a star.
Everything far comes near,
sang the moon to the star,
and everything near goes far.

First Summer

Here is your shadow-hand
holding the shadow of mine
as we drift along
over the grass
after a bee
or a butterfly.
You shout their names.
And here are the shadows
of your first words,
seen through the throat of a flower.

Here is a ball
bouncing away,
yellow and yellow,
under the sun;
your unwrapped voice
calling it back.
Here is a sun-hat,
blue and green,
a melting cone
in your fist.
And here is a message
faxed from the heart
to the lips,
as my shadow kneels again beside yours
for a shadow-kiss.

Time Transfixed

by René Magritte

In the Thinking Room
at Childhood Hall,
the brown clock ticks
with the sound of the kiss
that my Grandma makes
against my cheek
again and again
when we first meet
after a week
of all the hours
that the brown clock's tick
has kissed away
today, to-
morrow, yesterday

are all the same
to the plum steam-train
that I sometimes hear
in the Thinking Room
at Childhood Hall –
it has no passengers at all,
till I grow old enough
and tall
to climb aboard
the plum steam-train
and blow a kiss
as I chuff away to to-
morrow, yesterday, today.

Pestle and Mortar

Let's go to sea,
little daughter,
in a pestle and mortar.

I'll sit in the bowl
and you can row
over the water.

Then I'll take a turn
and watch you sleep
for three hours and a quarter.

Over the waves!
Aren't we brave!
Mother and daughter . . .

Al Ponte dei Giocattoli /
The Bridge of Toys

Don't worry about the gondola carrying away the dead boys
or the strange words the gondolier sings in a high-pitched voice
or the drumming crowd coming over the bridge in a wave of noise.

Don't worry about the masks: the small pale ones like white mice;
the beautiful ones with faces like Helen of Troy's;
the scarlet one with a slash for a mouth, the green one with a hook for a nose.

Don't worry about the man who takes out his teeth and rolls them for dice
or the skeletal hand that offers a weeping rose
or the dying bees underfoot or the absence of trees –

for you have your doll, isn't she nice,
you have your bear with his soft brown paws,
your wand, your balloon, your bouncing ball, and we stand
                         hand in hand on the Bridge of Toys.

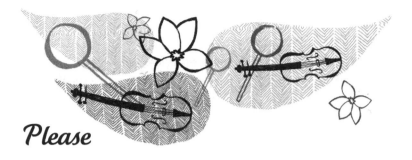

Please

Please.
Pretty please.
Pretty please with jam on top.
Pretty please with jam on top and ice-cream in the middle.

Please.
Beautiful please.
Beautiful please with a bunch of violets.
Beautiful please with a bunch of violets and a lollipop.

Please.
Gorgeous please.
Gorgeous please with perfume on.
Gorgeous please with perfume on and shiny shoes.

Please.
Lovely please.
Lovely please with silver wings.
Lovely please with silver wings and a magic wand.

Please.
Handsome please.
Handsome please with violins.
Handsome please with violins and moonlight.

Please.
Bonny please.
Bonny please with cheese on top.
Bonny please with cheese on top and pickle in the middle.

Please.
Comely please.
Comely please with a marzipan pig.
Comely please with a marzipan pig and a sugar mouse.

Please.
Photogenic please.
Photogenic please with ribbons on.
Photogenic please with ribbons on and ruby earrings.

Please.
Prepossessing please.
Prepossessing please with stardust.
Prepossessing please with stardust and wishes.

Please.
Pulchritudinous please.
Pulchritudinous please with pizza.
Pulchritudinous please with pizza and fairy tales.

Pleeeeeeeeeeeeeeeeease.

Your Dresses

I like your rain dress,
its strange, sad colour,
its small buttons like tears.

I like your fog dress,
how it swirls around you
when you dance on the lawn.

Your snow dress I like,
its million snowflakes
sewn together with a needle of ice.

But I love your thunderstorm dress,
its huge, dark petticoats,
its silver stitches flashing as you run away.

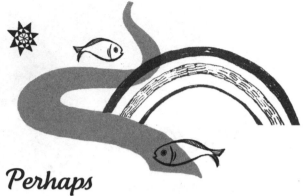

Perhaps

Perhaps a cloud, folded to
the four white squares of a handkerchief;

or a fistful of stars, dropped
in your purse for pocket money.

Perhaps a hurricane, smoothed
and hammered to a brooch;

or a field of grass, pleated,
hemmed and zipped for a kilt.

Perhaps a river, buckled
with bright, pewtery fish, for a belt;

or a rainbow, unpicked
to seven ribbons for your hair.

Perhaps the sea, flounced
and gathered into petticoats;

or the moon, framed, hung on your wall
for a mirror – look how lovely you are!

The Look

The heron's the look of the river.
The moon's the look of the night.
The sky's the look of forever.
Snow is the look of white.

The bees are the look of the honey.
The wasp is the look of pain.
The clown is the look of funny.
Puddles are the look of rain.

The whale is the look of the ocean.
The grave is the look of the dead.
The wheel is the look of motion.
Blood is the look of red.

The rose is the look of the garden.
The girl is the look of the school.
The snake is the look of the Gorgon.
Ice is the look of cool.

The clouds are the look of the weather.
The hand is the look of the glove.
The bird is the look of the feather.
You are the look of love.

Pay Me in Light

Pay me in light,
the sun's bonanza
flung in handfuls through the trees,
amber in green leaves; pay me
in the silver lining of the clouds,
a percentage of rain.

Pay me in light,
the newly minted moon,
the small-change stars,
the precious galaxy
sieved from space like gold,
a solitaire tear.

Pay me in light,
a candle's tongue in the dark's cheek,
sapphire lightning as we run for home,
your hand in mine, warm
as a small flame,
through lucky jackpot hail.

Loving

Go slow,
come soon,
eyes meet
on the moon.

Me here,
you far,
eyes meet
at a star.

Dark space
between us,
eyes meet
at Venus.

Whee!

I held my head in both my hands
and flung it through the air.
Blown by the wind, it flew away,
streaming out my hair.

The world, from high perspectives, looked
duller than ditchwater.
I rose above all mundane things –
Halley's Comet's daughter.

Higher than the flightpath of dreams
my cranium sped on;
while, down below, the people shrieked
'She's crazy! Head's gone.'

It's easy. Just shrug your shoulders,
turn your mind to the sky;
then throw your head like a basket-ball.
Wheee! Goodbye. Goodbye . . .

Lost

Left, left again, right, left, right, right again then left,
up, down, around and about, in, out, right, left, right . . .
Excellent, I'm lost; all alone on the lip of a wood –
sip, slurp, it's sucked me in, a morsel of white bread
in its dark mouth. The trees

                          are breathing quietly.
Who knows if a witch isn't a heap of leaves and old twigs,
hunched and sleeping under a bush? Or a bird
wasn't a girl like me, put under a spell and made to sing
on the branches of a silver birch

                              till another girl came
to take her place? I run away through the woods,
all voices miles away now. Who knows that a stone
isn't a toad with a jewel in its brain that hops away
when you touch it? Or a log isn't a sleeping prince

who'll suddenly stand, shaking the bugs and beetles
from his rusty hair? Lost is thrilling, my own scream
swooping away into the heart of this wood
as the night comes down, down, over my eyes
like a blindfold.

Jamjar

A girl in her garden peeped into a jamjar and fell inside.
She passed a wasp as she fell, it was licking
a smear of strawberry jam from the rim of the jar.
How far is the bottom? she cried as she fell.
Far, very far, drawled the wasp, *terribly far.*

Down she fell. The jar was a bell and her scream
was its tinkly, echoing ring. A green caterpillar
crawled up the outside glass of the jar, blinked
with its bulging alien eyes. *Help!* screeched the girl. *Help!*
Alas, it lisped, *there's no help in the whole wide world.*

On she hurled, into the well of the jar, till the opening
was a tiny star and dandelion clocks were silver planets
spinning in space. A spider hung from a thread
and peered at her face. *Throw me a rope!* she begged.
Not here, not now, it sneered, *nor any time or place.*

Bump. The jamjar's floor was snow and ice, stretching
for freezing miles. The girl skated away, all alone,
calling for home. White wolves ran in her tracks
under the hard stars. *Show me the way*, she sobbed.
No way to show, they howled, *and no way back.*

Then a hand picked up the jar; a mean squint eye swam
like a needlefish to the glass; poisonous breath clouded it over.
This will do for a vase, said a spiteful voice, as a Witch
filled up the jamjar with water, then stared in amazed,
glee in her eyes, at her swimming and brand new creature.

The Thief, the Priest
and the Golden Coin

Deep in the woods
in a hole
in a tree (a silver birch)
there's a golden coin
that was filched
by a thief from a church
and hidden there
as he fled
from a furious priest.

Wheesht.

All that remains to be said
is the thief was no gent,
the priest was no saint,
and the coin of gold
in the hole in the tree in the woods
has not yet been spent.

The Theft

Like it or lump it, I stole a large egg
from a nest and humped it home
in my bag. Natural swag. My plan
was to pierce each end of the shell
with a pin then blow what was in
outside and if something died . . .
too bad. I was that kind of a lad.

Long story short – I left the egg
on a shelf in my room, took my eye
off the ball, and was woken at dawn,
four days on, by the *peck-peck-peck*
of a beak and the *skrek-skrek-skrek*
of a claw from the well-cracked egg.
Out came a leg, feathery limbs, a head.

Now, I had no name for the thing
that stood in my room, but it knew mine
and squawked it out in an eggy croak,
the last trace of yolk running down like tears
from its eye. And it lived for a year
in my bottom bunk till the room stank
and they left my scram on a tray in the corridor.

Came home one night – it was gone,
the window flung, and a big yellow moon
like an egg in a non-stick pan outside.
I was sad, glad, felt bad – but not for long.
And if I could write, the story I'd tell is this.
And if I could sing, then this would be
my song. Don't steal, kids. It ain't worth it.

Snowball

More snow fell that week
than had fallen for thirty years.
The cold squeezed like a bully's hug
and made you grin at nothing.

Andrew Pond and Davy Rickers and me
went out,
three sprats,
into the white bite of the world.
We shared my balaclava.

And for an hour we chucked snowballs
at the windows on our estate;
spattered the pristine panes of Nelson Way,
powdered the gleaming glass up Churchill Drive,
until we got bored
and Andrew Pond's mitts from his Granny
shrank.

It was me who started it off,
that last snowball,
rolling it from the size of a 50p scoop
down Thatcher Hill
to the size of a spacehopper.
It creaked under my gloves as I pushed.
Then Andrew Pond and Davy Rickers joined in,
and we shoved the thing
the length of Wellington Road.
It groaned as it grew
and grew.

The size of a sleeping polar bear.
The size of an igloo.
The size,
by the time we turned the corner
into the road where I lived,
of a full moon –
the three of us astronauts.

The worst of it was
that Andrew Pond and Davy Rickers ran off,
leaving me
dwarfed and alarmed
by a planet of snow
on our front lawn.
It went so dark in our living-room,
I was later to hear,
that my mother thought there had been an eclipse.

And later that night –
after the terrible telling-off,
red-eyed,
supperless –
I stared from my bedroom window
at the enormity of my crime,
huge and luminous
under the ice-cold stars.
To tell the truth,
it was pride that I felt,
even though
I had to stop in for as long as it took
for the snowball to melt.

Walk

Confetti blows
outside the church
as I walk by.

Late summer wind
is dusty, dry.
No children play
in these long streets.

I stare at sweets
locked up behind
thick glass and steel
and want to cry.

The wedding guests
are somewhere else,
like happiness.

Don't Go to China

Don't go to China, it's too far, too far.
The slow boat will sail
till you're under a distant star, small
as a grain of rice, on the other side of the night
from where I pine, wondering what China's like.

Don't go there, the land of the yellow river,
the lantern moon, I can't come, today
or tomorrow, can't see you
crossing the little willow-pattern bridge
into a jasmine garden, going, gone. I can't follow.

Don't go to China. How will I know
where you are the length of the Great Wall
or where you sit in the rooms of steamy, fragrant tea,
or what you think as the red sun weeps
into the poppy fields? It's too far, too far.

The Invention of Rain

Rain first came
when the woman whose lovely face
was the sky
cried.

She thought of rain
for her sadness,
her sorrowful clouds.
The woman whose lonely voice
was the wind
howled.

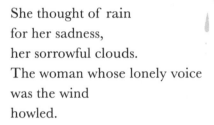

Then garden flowers
bowed their heads
under the soft-salt grief of the rain.

And an only child
stared down at them
through the thousand tears
of a window-pane.

How Emily Mercer (96) Grew Young

She stood in her nightgown staring out at the night. The moon
dissolved like a mint on the tongue. The sky grew light.

She walked again in the garden. Dead blooms straightened their stems
and flowered. A broken web re-strung itself like a necklace

to hang at the throat of a tree. *This is all for me*, thought Emily.
She left her sticks at the gate and ran for Wish-you-well Bridge.

The river talked with its mouth full, gleaming with bright ideas.
Goodbye, my dears! cried Emily. In she dived, her skin smooth

as a pearl, her white hair turning to red as she swam. She forgot
her grandchildren's names, her children, the tall dark handsome man

with the ring. Emily Mercer was always a girl who could swim. *Hi diddle dee
diddle di.* Aeroplanes in the buttery air turned to balloons in the sky.

A poacher up to his tricks on the bank noticed her splashing away.
Afterwards, when they asked, *She was young*, was all he could say.

Lightning Star

for May Duffy and her twelve grandchildren

I run at Lightning Star
and mount her back in one smooth jump;
then gallop her down Rising Brook,
wind in my face.
My pigtails thump.

My trusty steed.
I bend low to her ear
as trees rush by in camouflage.
We fly,
her coconut hooves racing with my heart
towards Moss Pit.

My piebald mount.
My equine brave.
My speed of light.
My warrior.
My Lightning Star.

It isn't far
to where we live –
21 Poplar Way –
so I slow down
as we approach the giant trees
which guard our neat estate.
I'm saddle-sore.
I stand up in my stirrups.

Time for bed.
I feel my horse's handlebars against my knees.
I hear my horse's neighing in my head.

The Maiden Names

I got a shock
hearing the grown-ups talk
to find that my Grandmother's name
wasn't her name at all,
only her married name.

I listened hard
till I heard
that the same was true
of Grandmother Two,
who had nearly been left
on the shelf
long ago
when she was called something else.

The maiden names
were their real names.
I spoke them aloud –
Mary Wallace, Agatha Hart,
Mary Wallace, Agatha Hart –
and saw them as maidens, lassies, girls
in their lost young worlds
with their own names.

Language inside me flared, burned,
then to my Mother I turned.

Peggy Guggenheim

co-written with Ella Duffy

Peggy, Peggy Guggenheim,
favourite drink Italian wine.
Peggy, Peggy Guggenheim,
favourite smell is turpentine.
Peggy, Peggy Guggenheim,
favourite jeans by Calvin Klein.
Peggy, Peggy Guggenheim,
favourite herb is lemon thyme.
Peggy, Peggy Guggenheim,
favourite fruit a Tuscan lime.
Peggy, Peggy Guggenheim,
favourite art Venetian mime.
Peggy, Peggy Guggenheim,
favourite tree a creeping vine.
Peggy, Peggy Guggenheim,
favourite statue free of grime.
Peggy, Peggy Guggenheim,
favourite poem has to rhyme
with Peggy, Peggy Guggenheim.

Venezia

Here today.
Gondolier tomorrow.

The Famous

What do the famous have for breakfast?
I think they have pale pink eggs
laid by rare birds, lightly boiled,
served by uniformed maids.

Then I think they have a bath, the famous,
in tubs with diamond taps.
They soak in perfumed lemonade
and their maids scrub their backs.

Then what? The famous get dressed, of course,
in gold and silver clothes
and go out for the day. They sail around
on the Thames in glass-bottomed boats,

waving at children on bridges,
while menservants fish for sturgeon
and scoop out the caviar with silver spoons
to feed to the famous for luncheon.

At bedtime the famous have stories
written specially by famous writers,
then they sleep and dream of being famous
in their sparkling pyjamas or nighties.

Deal with It

I saw some graffiti, it read
R.I.P. . . . Elvis is dead,
and although I think with my head,
I believe with my heart, grieve with it.
Elvis was King and I never heard him sing.

I saw a headline, it led
Elvis's death – pics of it,
and though I plan with my head,
I risk with my heart, wish with it.
Elvis could move and I never saw him groove.

I saw a badge, it said
Elvis is dead – deal with it,
and though I judge with my head,
I give with my heart, love with it.
Elvis lived and I never heard him live.

Moon

Scotland's moon
came up like a warrior's bronze shield
over the giant concrete and glass
of the new high-rise.

One hand made a fist
where a hard round coin
sweated its copper
into my skin.

The other
held onto my father's mother's hand.
Armstrong took
his one small step for a man

250,000 miles
over our heads –
or in a Hollywood studio,
as Grandma scornfully said.

Elvis! Shakespeare! Picasso! Virginia Woolf!

I had knowledge in my youth;
did the experiment, wrote the proof;
waved my hand whenever asked,
hollered an answer, top of the class, truth –
Elvis! Shakespeare! Picasso! Virginia Woolf!

I knew the score in my youth;
Beethoven's Ninth, Mozart's Flute;
classical, opera, all that jazz,
sang out the answer, class, aloof –
Elvis! Shakespeare! Picasso! Virginia Woolf!

Time of day, knew it, in my youth;
twenty-four seven from my mooth
came Physics, History, Spanish, Maths,
answers flew around the class, whoosh –
Elvis! Shakespeare! Picasso! Virginia Woolf!

No problemo in my youth;
ça va? Merci. Fermez la bouche.
Sic transit gloria; amo, amas,
I barked the answer, best in class, woof –
Elvis! Shakespeare! Picasso! Virginia Woolf!

So when questioned in my youth
re: blue shoes, shrews, cubes, own gaff,
I was never going to pass,
had the answers, showed my class –
the king, best, genius and herself . . .
Elvis! Shakespeare! Picasso! Virginia Woolf!

The Hat

I was on Chaucer's head when he said He was a verray,
parfit gentil knyght, and tossed me into the air. I landed
on Thomas Wyatt's hair as he thought They fle from me
that sometyme did me seek, then left me behind in an Inn.
Sir Philip Sidney strolled in, picked me up, saying
My true love hath my hart and I have his, then hoopla'd me
straight onto William Shakespeare's head as he said
Tell me where is fancie bred, and passed me along
to John Donne, who was wearing me as he sang Go
and catch a falling star, but handed me on to one leaving
the bar, name of Herbert, George, who wore me up top
like a halo, murmured Love bade me welcome, yet my soul
drew back, then lay me dreamily down at the end of a pew
in a church. I was there for a while, dwelling on heaven
and hell, till Andrew Marvell arrived, said Had we
but World enough and Time, and filled me up to the brim
with blooms to give to a girl. She kept the flowers,
but handed me on to warm the crown of a balding chap,
named Milton, John, who sported me the day he happened
to say They also serve who only stand and wait,
then threw me over a gate. I fell in the path of Robert Herrick,

who scooped me up with a shout of Gather ye rosebuds
while ye may! and later gave me away to Dryden, John,
who tried me on for size, saying None but the brave
deserves the fair, then let me drop. I was soon picked up
by a bloke, Alexander Pope, who admitted the gen'ral rule
that every poet's a fool with cheerful grace, then tilted me
over the face of Christopher Smart, who loved his cat, said
For first he looks upon his forepaws to see if they
are clean, and let the kitty kip in myself, The Hat. I was saved
from that by William Blake, who liked the extra inch or two
I gave to his height as he bawled out Tyger, Tyger, burning
bright in the forests of the night, then bartered me
for the price of a mutton pie to Robbie Burns, who stared
in the mirror, grunted O, wad some Pow'r the giftie gie us
to see oursels as others see us! and threw me out
of the window. S.T. Coleridge passed, muttering Water,
water, everywhere, nor any drop to drink, and bore me
off to the Lakes to give as a gift to Wordsworth. Will
wore me to keep out the cold on a stroll when, all at once,
he said that he saw a crowd, a host of golden daffodils,
and lobbed me high with delight! It was late at night
when Byron came, mad, bad, bit of a lad, insisting So,
we'll go no more a roving, as he kicked me into a tree.
A breeze blew me gently down from my branch to flop
onto Shelley's head as he said O, Wind, if Winter comes,
can Spring be far behind? But Keats sneaked up,
snatched me away, wore me the night he claimed
I cannot see what flowers are at my feet, and left me
snagged on a bush in the gathering dark of a park.
John Clare came along, shouted I am, yet what I am
none cares or knows, and jammed me down
on his puzzled brow as he made for the open road.
Then Tennyson, Alfred, Lord, thundered past on a horse
and yanked me off, yelled Into the Valley of Death

rode the six hundred! I flew from his head as he galloped
away, and settled on Browning's crown as he said This
to you – my moon of poets, and got down on one knee
to present Little Me to Elizabeth Barrett. I liked it up there,
snug on her shiny hair, as she cooed How do I love thee,
let me count the ways, but she handed me down
for Emily Brontë to wear on the moors as she wailed
Fifteen wild Decembers from those brown hills have melted
into Spring, then a blast of wind blew me to the edge of the sea
where Matthew Arnold wore me to keep off the spray
when he said Listen! You hear the grating roar of pebbles
which the waves draw back, and lobbed me over the foam
like a boy with a stone. I bobbed away like a boat,
till fished from the drink on t'other side of the pond
by Whitman, Walt, who wrung me dry and flung me high
as he bawled Behold, I do not give lectures or a little
charity, when I give I give myself, and sent me on with a kiss
to Emily Dickinson. She popped me into a hat-box, along
with a note that read This is my letter to the world,
that never wrote to me, then posted me over land and sea
to Christina Rossetti, who used me to keep the blazing sun
from her face as she asked Does the road wind up-hill
all the way? The reply being yes, she considered it best
to hand me to Hopkins, Gerard Manley, whose head
I adorned as he warmly intoned Glory be to God
for dappled things, but I fell to the ground as he stared
at the sky. Thomas Hardy came sauntering by, spied me
and tried me, said I am the family face; flesh perishes,
I live on, and tossed me to one who stood on his own
by a tree – Housman, A. E. He sported me, saying Lads
in their hundreds to Ludlow come in for the fair, but lost me,
while arm-wrestling there in a bar, to Kipling, Rudyard,
who fiddled with me the day he pronounced If you can meet
with triumph and disaster and treat those two impostors

just the same, then carelessly left me behind in the back
of a cab. Next in was an Irish chap, W. B. Yeats, who gave
the driver a tip, carried me off to wear at a tilt on his head
as he said Tread softly because you tread on my dreams,
so Charlotte Mew bore me away, murmured no year
has been like this that has just gone by, and started to cry.
A train sighed by. Edward Thomas leaned out, said
Yes, I remember Adlestrop, and lifted me up, but a cold wind
blew me Wilfred Owen's way; he turned me sadly round
and around in his hands and asked What passing-bells
for these who die as cattle? then hurled me back
at the wind. I was seized as I flew by Ezra Pound,
who wore me out and about, saying Winter is
icummen in, Lhude sing Goddamn! then posted me
into the safety deposit box of the bank where T. S. Eliot
worked. April, he said, is the cruellest month, and used me
to keep off the rain, leaving me lying behind on a bench
when the sun came out. I was found by MacDiarmid, Hugh,
and was warming the egg of his head when he said I'll ha'e
nae hauf-way hoose, but aye be whaur extremes meet –
then dropped me down at the feet of Lawrence, D. H.,
who picked me up and was modelling me as he mused
I never saw a wild thing sorry for itself, then chucked me over
to Robert Graves. He pulled me low on his head and said
There's a cool web of language winds us in, then began
to nod off. I was pinched from his brow by Riding, Laura,
who was trying me on as she thought The wind suffers
of blowing, the sea suffers of water, then squashed me
down onto Dylan Thomas's curls. Do not, he said,
go gentle into that good night, then sold me on
for the price of a pint to Louis MacNeice. He wore me
when he said World is crazier and more of it
than we think, then decided to give me to Auden, W. H.
He was delighted, wore me all night, said the desires

of the heart are as crooked as corkscrews, but left me
behind the next day in the loo. John Betjeman found me,
smoothed, dusted-down me, and popped me on
as he trilled Come, friendly bombs, then flopped me on
to the head of Philip Larkin, who cycled past, saying
Man hands on misery to man, then stopped at a church
and handed me on by the graves to Stevie Smith,
who wore me on holiday with her aunt, where she said
I was much further out than you thought, and not waving
but drowning. I was all at sea, till Elizabeth Bishop deftly
hooked me, said I caught a tremendous fish, and held him
beside the boat, then left me behind on an airport seat
for Robert Lowell to find and put on for the flight over
to England. He arrived and declared Everywhere,
giant finned cars nose forward like fish, and gave me
to Sylvia Plath. Dying, she said, is an art like everything else,
and left me to Hughes, Ted, man in black, who growled
with a sudden sharp hot stink of fox it enters the dark hole
of the head . . . but whose head, whose head, whose head,
whose head, whose head, whose will I settle on next?

Picasso's Blue Paintings

1. PAINT

Paint can be a mother's hand
touching a child,
brush-strokes turning to fingers.

Or paint is a child's blue eyes,
bright on the canvas,
on the brink of seeing.

Or a mother's lips. Look.
Surely she's about to bend her head
and kiss?

2. THE PEACH

I am a juicy peach.
These people are starving.

One bite each till I'm gone –
that's the bargain.

How blue they are!
But I glow, glow, like a moon.

I am not sad like them,
though I'm going soon.

3. EYES

Her one blind eye
is filled with sky.
It cannot see.
It cannot cry.

Her other eye
can watch and spy
until it sees
enough to cry.

4. THE BLUE FAMILY

The Blues, the Blues,
have lost their shoes.
Where can they be?

Here's news, here's news,
the family's shoes
are lost at sea.

5. BLUE

Blue like the sound of a saxophone
in the rain.
Blue like waving goodbye
to an aeroplane.
Blue like a lost thought
trapped in the brain.
Blue like the last of the light
in a country lane.
Blue like a bruise on the skin,
a tender pain.
Blue like the faraway whistle
of a train.
Blue like shadows trapped
in a locked case.
Blue like the empty, endless miles
of space.
Blue like the vacant chair
that was your place.
Blue like loneliness,
its silent grace.
Blue like boredom,
its slow pace.
Blue like the light in the tears that fall
on your face.

6. THE CLOWNS

Away from the circus,
the sawdust,
the silly red noses,

the glum clowns
gaze down
in their blue poses.

7. BLUE WOMAN

One day, my face froze
with sorrow.

Bereavement filled my head
till I turned to a blue stone.

At least I do not weep,
I do not moan.

I will look like this
tomorrow, and tomorrow.

8. MISSING

I miss you so much
I have turned into Art.

Inside my head is an orchestra
constantly tuning up. Listen.

My closed, tired eyes are reading
a poem as long as a river.

And my body is blue and grey paint.
And you are the artist.

9. BLUE ROOM

I wish we lived high up
in that blue room
at the end of the blue street,
with our heads in the blue-grey clouds,
and blue life sweet.

The Architect of Cheese

(Stilton! Thou shouldst be given at this hour!)

He started small, with half-a-pound of Brie
and made an egg-cup for Mama on Mother's Day.
The tray. The single rose. The cup of tea.
The piping hot boiled egg.

                        At University,
in Philadelphia, crème de la crème,
he won the Graduate Prize
for fashioning a chamber pot from Danish Blue.
The fluff under the bed. The softening rim.
The Midas urine. (Poo.)

Inspired, he set up shop alone
and spent six months on modelling a mobile phone
from Emmental.
The numbers One to Zero neatly holed.
The cheesey screensaver. The mouldy texts.
The minging ringing tones.
Next year, he made another one from Feta,
which sold better.

He fell madly in love
and, for the girl his future happiness
was built on, determined
to design a wedding-ring from Stilton.
The best man's best suit's pong. The two *I do*'s.
The something old, new, borrowed, something blue.

He went from strength to strength; made
Mozzarella um-ber-ellas, Cheddar beds,
one cathedral built from Stinking Bishop,
a bridge made out of Pont le Veque,
re-built the whole of Leicester city centre, red.

And when he died,
the coffin that he lay in was Halloumi
and every mourner at his funeral
was gloomy.

A Week as My Home Town

MONDAY:

Rain. I'm the Library, round-shouldered, my stone brow
frowning at pigeons, my windows steamed up
like spectacles, my swing doors tut-tutting, my bricks
beginning to feel the damp.

                    Readers come,
whispering and coughing, shaking umbrellas
at the back of my yawning marble throat. My old lifts sigh
up and down, up and down, up and down. *Ssssshhh*.

Books flap in my head like wings, poems, wings.

TUESDAY:

Weak sun. I'm the Park. My trees
wear last night's rain like jewels.
I wake. Birds brush my tangled, leafy hair, I gargle
with a water-fountain, admire my green face
in the mirror of a small lake.

                    My thoughts
are a game of bowls, slow and calm.
I hum to myself in a lawnmower bass
among my bright municipal flowers,
my namesake benches.

WEDNESDAY:

Fog. Museum, me. I hark back
to the past for endless hours, hoard
bronze coins in glass wallets, keep
long-gone summer butterflies on pins.

I remember things, pick
over old bones, look under cold stones,
check the names of the Kings and Queens
who sat on the gold thrones.

My stained-glass eyes stare inwards.

THURSDAY:

Sunshine. I'm the Main Road.
I lie on my back, stretch out
my side-street arms, wriggle
my alley toes, my mews fingers.

My throat is a tunnel
under a river. I burp cars
into the sparkling daylight,
belch lorries and juggernauts.

My heart's a roundabout,
in love with the next town.

FRIDAY:

Grey cloud. I'm the Cinema, daydream
all day, can't sleep at night, hear

voices . . . *to infinity and beyond* . . . see
faces . . . *I'm all aloooone* . . . smell

popcorn . . . *please sir, can I have*
some more . . . They shine a light

in my eyes, prod at my plush red teeth.
I want to phone home. I'll be right here.

SATURDAY:

Frost. I'm the Disco. My neon lips
pout at the shivery night. My heart thumps
so loud the queue outside can hear it.

I wear light, glitterballs, lasers, strobe,
too much perfume. One day I'll give up smoking.
If anyone asks if I'm dancing, I'm dancing.

SUNDAY:

Snow. I'm the Church,
stone-flags for my shoes,
for my hat a steeple.

I kneel by the side of the graves
and sob with my bells.
Where are the people?

The Rings

With this ring of lead
I me wed
to grey skies, rainfall, writing days.

With this wooden ring
I me wed
to forests, grim tales, ancient things.

With this ring of stone
I me wed
to mountains, echoes, vanishings.

With this silver ring
I me wed
to rivers, moonlight, midnight hours.

With this ring of gold
I me wed
to meadows, sunsets, wishing wells.

With this ruby ring
I me wed
to passion, poems, magic spells.

The Written Queen

I stare through my window.
The Written Queen stands outside
in the rain in her green robes,
tall as a tree, sad as the dripping leaves.
She is waiting for me.

I go to sleep. The Written Queen
breathes in the dark room,
soft as shade, hushed, black
as a closed and dreaming eye.
She is watching me.

I go out, pass under
the curtseying trees, the doffed clouds,
and see the Written Queen
at the end of the avenue.
She is beckoning me.

I read – her hand's shadow
falls on the words of my book.
I dance – her tapping shoe
follows the curves of my foot.
She is devoted to me.

I take up paper and pen
and write her, line by line, once
upon a time. Here is her sceptre, her crown,
her palace, here is her throne.
She is all mine.

Haikus from Basho

1

In rainy weather
even the cheeky monkey
needs an umbrella.

2

From the ancient pond
with a spring and leap and splash
burps a new green frog.

3

When friends say goodbye
forever, it's like wild geese
erased by the clouds.

4

I gaze at the moon.
Without the gathering clouds
I would hurt my neck.

5

Tall summer grasses
stand at ease now in the fields
where the soldiers fell.

6

The pale butterfly
gently perfumes her frail wings
in an orchid bath.

7

This lonely poet
walks down a long empty road
into autumn dusk.

8

The morning after
the night before, the firefly
is only a bug.

No Stone Unturned

Under the pebble caressed by a thumb,
an ant with a crumb.
Under the stone covered in moss,
the keys to a house.
Under the brick warmed by the sun,
a cool worm.
Under the rock on a desert plain,
a thimble of rain.
Under the boulder dark in a field,
a Roman shield.

Under the pebble picked from a beach,
a damp niche.
Under the stone on a garden wall,
nothing at all.
Under the brick on top of a skip,
a school cap.
Under the rock where they buried the gold,
an empty hole.
Under the boulder sealing a tomb,
a room.

Under the pebble spied for a sling,
a gold ring.
Under the stone slung at a steeple,
a black beetle.
Under the brick on the country road,
a green toad.
Under the rock sheltered by trees,
brown bees.
Under the boulder blocking the ford,
a silver sword.

Under the pebble smooth as a bead,
a seed.
Under the stone black as a hat,
a rat.
Under the brick tied to the boat,
a note.
Under the rock south of the lake,
a snake.
Under the boulder high on the hill,
a skull.

Under the pebble sore in a shoe,
glue.
Under the stone in the wishing-well bucket,
a ticket.
Under the brick in a spring flower-bed,
a bud.
Under the rock in the waterfall,
a caul.
Under the boulder rolled in the cave,
poor Dave.

Under the pebble saved for a lover,
clover.
Under the stone about to be chucked,
muck.
Under the brick warming the sheets,
treats.
Under the rock anchoring a ship,
fish and chips.
Under the boulder obstructing the pass,
grass.

Under the pebble washed up by the sea,
a flea.
Under the stone on the teacher's desk,
a test.
Under the brick in a prison cell,
a file.
Under the rock where the seagulls beg,
an egg.
Under the boulder aglow on the Moon,
a dish and a spoon.

Under the pebble safe in a pocket,
a locket.
Under the stone in Picasso's gaze,
a Cubist maze.
Under the brick in a garden shed,
something dead.
Under the rock in the Punishment Block,
more rock.
Under the boulder in the Modern Art Gallery,
talented Valerie.

Under the pebble kicked in the street,
a centipede's feet.
Under the stone skimmed on the ocean,
motion.
Under the brick on the flap of a tent,
cement.
Under the rock transformed by a wizard,
a lizard.
Under the boulder hewn like a throne,
a mobile phone.

Under the pebble used as a pawn,
a prawn.
Under the stone scraped with initials,
thistles.
Under the brick marking the goal,
a mole.
Under the rock in the castle grounds,
a million pounds.
Under the boulder on the ocean floor,
a ragged claw.

Under the pebble cherished for years,
dried tears.
Under the stone at the end of the garden,
a pardon.
Under the brick at the edge of the pond,
a wand.
Under the rock in the heart of the woods,
stolen goods.
Under the boulder sunk in the swamp,
a lamp.

Under the pebble pawed by a kitten,
a mitten.
Under the stone silvered by ice,
mice.
Under the brick in the builders' yard,
a pack of cards.
Under the rock in the cemetery,
a flask of tea.
Under the boulder next to the Nile,
a crocodile.

Under the pebble dropped by a girl,
a pearl.
Under the stone on the banks of the Mersey,
a red jersey.
Under the brick in the criminals' den,
a golden pen.
Under the rock in London Zoo,
a sleeping gnu.
Under the boulder lit up by lightning,
somebody frightening.

Under the pebble placed on a dish,
a wish.
Under the stone kept on a shelf,
an elf.
Under the brick in the gardener's hut,
a tough nut.
Under the rock in the wilds of Peru,
an Inca shoe.
Under the boulder out on the patio,
a pistachio.

Under the pebble sewn in a dress,
an address.
Under the stone in a hole in a tree,
a plea.
Under the brick holding open the gate,
a time and a place and a date.
Under the rock in the shady nook,
a poetry book.
Under the boulder rolled in a ditch,
a witch.

Under the pebble touched by a baby,
a daisy.
Under the stone in a cowboy's boot,
a cheroot.
Under the brick from Ancient Greece,
a fragment of fleece.
Under the rock where the lighthouse flickers,
a mermaid's knickers.
Under the boulder huge on the mountain,
an underground fountain.

Under the pebble worn by the weather,
purple heather.
Under the stone in the shape of a heart,
a dart.
Under the brick on the window-sill,
a glazier's bill.
Under the rock tourists come and go,
talking of Michelangelo.
Under the boulder, hissy and fussed,
Sisyphus.

Under the pebble next to a thistle,
a whistle.
Under the stone kicked by a horse,
a purse.
Under the brick tethering a balloon,
a macaroon.
Under the rock where the ship went aground,
the drowned.
Under the boulder dragged by an ox,
a fox.

Under the pebble in a puddle,
a bubble.
Under the stone in a storm,
a corm.
Under the brick in the fog,
a frog.
Under the rock in the rain,
a drain.
Under the boulder in space,
space.

Under the boulder next to the loch,
a rock.
Under the rock inscribed *R.I.P. MICK*,
a brick.
Under the brick, fossiled with fishbone,
a stone.
Under the stone, causing no trouble,
a pebble.
Under the pebble, caressed by a thumb,
another ant with a crumb.

A Child's Sleep

I stood at the edge of my child's sleep
hearing her breathe;
although I could not enter there,
I could not leave.

Her sleep was a small wood,
perfumed with flowers;
dark, peaceful, sacred,
acred in hours.

And she was the spirit that lives
in the heart of such woods;
without time, without history,
wordlessly good.

I spoke her name, a pebble dropped
in the still night,
and saw her stir, both open palms
cupping their soft light;

then went to the window. The greater dark
outside the room
gazed back, maternal, wise,
with its face of moon.

Night Writing

Only a neat margin of moonlight
there at the curtain's edge.
The room like a dark page.
I lie in bed.

Silence is ink.
The sound of my breath dips in
and out. So I begin
night writing. The stars type themselves
far out in space.

Who would guess,
to look at my sleeping face,
the rhymes and tall tales I invent?
Here be dragons; children lost
in the wood; three wishes; the wicked
and the good.

Read my lips.
The small hours are poems.
Dawn is a rubber.